THE COUNSELLOR'S GUIDE TO PERSONALITY

Professional Handbooks in Counselling and Psychotherapy

This series of professional handbooks is designed for trainees as well as practitioners in the field of psychological therapy, counselling, emotional wellbeing and mental health. It focuses on key areas of practice interest and training need.

The books are characterised by:

- their pluralistic and undogmatic approach to theory – theoretically informed, they maintain a flexible view about what works best for whom
- their practical stance – the books all focus on the guidance professionals need in order to optimise their skills and effectiveness
- their easy-to-use format – they are clearly structured in order to aid navigation and employ devices such as vignettes, transcripts, checklists and questions to support the reader in deepening their understanding of the main issues.

Published

Rowan Bayne
The Counsellor's Guide to Personality: Understanding Preferences, Motives and Life Stories

Robert Bor, Sheila Gill, Riva Miller and Amanda Evans
Counselling in Health Care Settings: A Handbook for Practitioners

Susy Churchill
The Troubled Mind: A Handbook of Therapeutic Approaches to Psychological Distress

Gill Jones and Anne Stokes
Online Counselling: A Handbook for Practitioners

Forthcoming

Robert Bor and Anne Stokes
Setting Up in Independent Practice: A Handbook for Therapy and Psychology Practitioners

The Counsellor's Guide to Personality

Understanding Preferences, Motives and Life Stories

Rowan Bayne

© Rowan Bayne 2013

All rights reserved. No reproduction, copy or transmission of this publication may be made without written permission.

No portion of this publication may be reproduced, copied or transmitted save with written permission or in accordance with the provisions of the Copyright, Designs and Patents Act 1988, or under the terms of any licence permitting limited copying issued by the Copyright Licensing Agency, Saffron House, 6–10 Kirby Street, London EC1N 8TS.

Any person who does any unauthorized act in relation to this publication may be liable to criminal prosecution and civil claims for damages.

Rowan Bayne has asserted his right to be identified as the author of this work in accordance with the Copyright, Designs and Patents Act 1988.

First published 2013 by
PALGRAVE MACMILLAN

Palgrave Macmillan in the UK is an imprint of Macmillan Publishers Limited, registered in England, company number 785998, of Houndmills, Basingstoke, Hampshire RG21 6XS.

Palgrave Macmillan in the US is a division of St Martin's Press LLC, 175 Fifth Avenue, New York, NY 10010.

Palgrave Macmillan is the global academic imprint of the above companies and has companies and representatives throughout the world.

Palgrave® and Macmillan® are registered trademarks in the United States, the United Kingdom, Europe and other countries.

ISBN 978-0-230-28244-5   ISBN 978-1-137-29720-4 (eBook)

DOI 10.1007/978-1-137-29720-4

A catalogue record for this book is available from the British Library.

A catalog record for this book is available from the Library of Congress.

10 9 8 7 6 5 4 3 2 1
22 21 20 19 18 17 16 15 14 13

Contents

List of Figures and Tables	x
Preface	xii
Acknowledgements	xv
Introduction	xvi

1	**Personality and Counselling**	**1**
	McAdams' integrative model of personality	1
	Domain one: traits (or preferences)	2
	Domain two: motives	3
	Domain three: life stories	3
	How personality theory is important in counselling	4
	Research on the effectiveness of counselling	4
	Increasing self-awareness	5
	Improving the counselling relationship	8
	As a new perspective on client problems	9
	Psychological type or preference theory	9
	The concept of 'preference'	9
	The concept of 'psychological type'	11
	Five factor theory or the 'Big Five'	13
	Reframing anxiety as two preferences	14
	Comparing preference theory and the Big Five	15
	Validity	15
	Tone	16
	Versatility	17
	Personality development	18
	Personality change	20
	An apparent exception	21

Developing the ten preferences	22
Four general principles	22
Strategies	23
An overview of how counsellors can use preference theory	24
Conclusions	25
Appendix: Summary of single-letter abbreviations for the ten preferences	26

2 Increasing Self-awareness 1: Discovering the Preferences — 27

Four general principles for discovering the preferences — 28
Two case studies — 29
Strategies for helping clients discover their preferences in a counselling session — 30
  Be clear about the meaning of each preference — 31
  Consider whether pressures early in life or now are relevant — 39
  Consider using brief exercises — 39
  Consider using Keirsey's ideas about the four temperaments — 39
  Consider using a questionnaire — 42
  Read brief descriptions of the whole types — 42
  Read longer descriptions — 43
Two extra strategies for discovering the preferences outside a counselling session — 46
  Experiment with behaving as if you have each preference — 46
  Ask people who know you well — 46
Replies to questions about preference theory and the process of discovering preferences — 46

3 Increasing Self-awareness 2: Discovering Motives — 49

Motives and the four temperaments — 50
Motives and the preferences — 52
Motives for becoming a counsellor — 60
The 'good counsellor' — 61
Motives and your choice of counselling model or models — 61
Discovering personal strivings — 65
Two general methods for discovering motives — 67
Values and strengths — 68

4 Improving the Counselling Relationship — 70

Matching counsellors and clients — 71
  Four 'languages' — 71
  Stages of change — 72

The authentic chameleon issue	73
Collecting feedback and the skill of immediacy	74
Notes on communicating with clients of each preference	75
Clients who prefer Extraversion (E) or Introversion (I)	75
Clients who prefer Sensing (S) or Intuition (N)	76
Clients who prefer Thinking (T) or Feeling (F)	77
Clients who prefer Judging (J) or Perceiving (P)	78
Clients who prefer Calm (C) or Worrying (W)	78
Two case studies	79
An ISFJ client	79
An ENFP client	79
The core counselling qualities	80
Acceptance	80
Empathy	82
Genuineness	84
Marketing yourself as a counsellor	85
Your counselling room	86

5 **How Personality Can Affect Clients' Problems with Love and Work** — 88

The preferences and communication: problems and strategies	89
The four temperaments and communication	92
Some problems with love	92
Client 1: Love bothers me: how do I know...?	92
Client 2: Which love style is best for me?	94
Client 3: We kiss so differently...	94
Client 4: Why do I take so long to recover...?	95
A note on potential problems between people with the same preferences	95
Client 5: I want a good relationship that lasts...	96
Client 6: I feel such a bad mother...	97
Some problems with work	98
Client 1: What work would suit me?	98
Client 2: How can I improve my CV?	100
Client 3: How can I improve my interview technique?	100
Client 4: I've been late too often...	100
A note on time 'management'	101
Client 5: We have a new trainer and I can't follow him at all...	102

	Client 6: I've been made redundant and I'm struggling...	103
	Client 7: I rarely speak in meetings...	103
6	**How Personality Can Affect Clients' Problems with Health**	**104**
	Physical health	106
	Client 1: I'm tired all the time...	106
	A note on stress	107
	Client 2: I want to lose weight and I've tried so many different ways...	109
	Client 3: I know I need to do more exercise but it's so boring...	111
	Client 4: I've got Parkinson's...	112
	A note on loss	113
	Mental health	114
	A note on personality disorders	114
	A note on ADHD and ADD	115
	A note on dementia	116
7	**Extended Case Studies of Personality Development**	**118**
	Type development from an ESTJ perspective, by Jean Kummerow	119
	Developing my preferences and non-preferences, by an INFPC	128
	Love of words	128
	Love of sport	129
	Appealing and repelling activities	129
	Looking for romantic love	129
	Time alone	130
	Other preferences and non-preferences	130
8	**Increasing Self-awareness 3: Discovering Life Stories**	**131**
	How and when to suggest exploring life stories	132
	Some methods for exploring life stories	133
	Scripts	133
	The life story interview	134
	Self-defining memories	135
	Archetypes	135
	Analysing and reconstructing life stories	137
	Concluding comment	139

Further Resources	140
Books and articles	140
Other Resources	140
References	142
Index	151

List of Figures and Tables

FIGURES

2.1 Temperament stick figures — 41

TABLES

0.1 A three-stage model of integrative counselling — xii
1.1 The variation of McAdams' model used in this book and related personality theories and concepts — 4
1.2 A model of self and self-awareness — 6
1.3 Brief descriptions of the preferences (when developed) — 11
1.4 An indication of the meanings of the factors in Big Five theory — 14
1.5 Personality and examples of consequential outcomes — 16
1.6 Comparing the tone of four of the preferences and the broadly equivalent factors: some examples — 17
1.7 Strategies for developing preferences — 24
2.1 Some characteristics associated with preferences for E and I — 33
2.2 Some characteristics associated with preferences for S and N — 34
2.3 Some characteristics associated with preferences for T and F — 35
2.4 Some characteristics associated with preferences for J and P — 36

2.5	Some characteristics associated with preferences for C and W	37
2.6	Very brief descriptions of the 16 types	44
3.1	Examples of core motives in the four temperaments	51
3.2	Gordon Lawrence's descriptions of the 16 MBTI 'types', emphasising motives and values	53
3.3	Main motives proposed for sets of three preferences, based on type dynamics and adapted from K. Myers and Kirby (1994)	59
3.4	The ten preferences and associated strengths and weaknesses to work on for counsellors	62
3.5	Stages of counselling and the preferences most relevant to each	63
3.6	MBTI preferences (%) of experienced counsellors (N = 123)	64
3.7	Preferences (%) of experienced CBT counsellors (N = 23)	65
4.1	Some negative perceptions of each preference	81
4.2	Three meanings of genuineness	84
4.3	The preferences and writing	86
5.1	Opposed preferences and central problems in communication	90
5.2	General ways of managing problems in communicating between people of opposing preferences	91
5.3	Eight main styles of loving	93
5.4	Four pairs of preferences and time	102
5.5	Eight preferences and aspects of learning styles associated with them	102
6.1	The preferences and what tends to be experienced as particularly stressful	107
6.2	The four temperaments and reactions to stress	107
6.3	The preferences and ways of coping with stress	108
6.4	Personality characteristics associated with eight sets of preferences	109
6.5	The four temperaments and losing weight	110
6.6	Eight sets of preferences and favourite kinds of exercise	112
8.1	Examples of archetypes and associated qualities	137

Preface

I have written this book for practitioners and students of counselling, psychotherapy and coaching of all the main orientations, though most obviously for counsellors who use an integrative model. However, the integrative counselling model (see Table 0.1), which I taught for many years, recognises the value of other models and I hope therefore that the book will be useful to practitioners from other orientations too. Counsellors who specialise in a particular orientation may also find useful insights.

For example, Stage 1 of the model is the core qualities of acceptance, empathy and genuineness – person-centred counselling. Of course, many person-centred counsellors believe that these qualities are always sufficient, whereas in the above model they are sometimes sufficient and sometimes not, hence the phrase 'if necessary' next to Stages 2 and 3 in Table 0.1. Either way, the applications of personality theory to self-awareness and the counselling relationship in this book can be seen as helpful to person-centred counsellors.

Similarly, the central personality theory in this book was developed from Carl Jung's (1923) ideas about 'psychological types' by Isabel Myers

Table 0.1 A three-stage model of integrative counselling

Stage 1: Support
The counsellor accepts and empathises with the client and is genuine. The client explores their reaction to one or more problems.

Stage 2 (if necessary): Challenge or new perspectives
The counsellor suggests, or helps the client suggest, a new way of looking at the problem, then helps the client explore their reaction to this new perspective.

Stage 3 (if necessary): Set goals and agree action
The counsellor helps the client decide what to do and how.

Source: Based on Hill (2009), Egan (2010) and others.

(e.g., Myers with Myers 1980; Myers et al. 1998). There is a more psychodynamic grouping in contemporary psychological type theory and practice represented by Naomi Quenk (e.g., 1996, 2002), and a more humanistic one represented by Judy Provost (1993). However, this book is definitely humanistic in approach so the link is a tenuous one, at least for classical psychodynamic counsellors and therapists.

Returning to my background, I was a counsellor trainer (at the University of East London and its predecessors) for 32 years and before that an occupational psychologist in the Civil Service (with an office in Whitehall!) where I developed a particular interest in training selection interviewers. Before the Civil Service I was a postgraduate student at Aberdeen University, studying authenticity and self-disclosure. As a counsellor I have worked mainly with clients who had 'problems with living' such as mild depression, sexual jealousy, fear of HIV and study problems, and occasionally with clients with more severe mental health problems such as 'borderline personality disorder' and clinical depression.

My interest in personality theory began quite early. When I was 12 or 13 I drew a diagram of my own personality which, in a generous interpretation, can be seen as depicting Rogers' and Maslow's theories. It was three circles, like a dartboard, with the centre one labelled 'real me', and I was concerned about whether each ring and particularly the central circle was 'hard' or 'soft'. Gender stereotypes and a wish for authenticity were therefore early influences and motives.

During all those years, I have been helped (stimulated, provoked, encouraged) by many hundreds of students, colleagues and other people. It seems invidious to name individuals and impractical to name everyone I'd like to, but I will single out six people as especially important for the topic of this book. In chronological order they are:

- Albert E. Hughes, a psychoanalyst and author who I spent many hours with when I was a young psychology student discussing unorthodox methods of personality assessment – graphology, palmistry and a projective test called the Szondi.
- Phillip Greenway, a psychology lecturer who probably saved my PhD by saying about a draft (the third, I think, and my supervisors had formally advised me to stop): 'It's basically OK and at the right level of thinking but needs more signposts.'
- Francesca Inskipp, who taught me basic counselling skills and much more when we 'co-led' (she was the actual leader) a small group in my first year as a psychology lecturer.

- Ian Horton, for teaching me so much about counselling and counsellor training.
- Gordon Lawrence, who led my qualifying course on the MBTI (Myers-Briggs Type Indicator), for being a model of calm, clear thinking and for his warm support of my writing. He felt like a father figure. Sadly, he died on 14 December 2010 and I dedicate this book to him.
- Katherine Bayne, for being very supportive, a skilful and patient word processor and a splendid example of her preferences.

Acknowledgements

A very warm thank you to Carolyn Lawrence and CAPT (the Center for Applications of Psychological Type) for permission to include Gordon Lawrence's descriptions of the 16 types in Chapter 3; and to Hile Rutledge, CEO and owner of OKA, for permission to use the unpublished stick figures of the four temperaments and the very brief descriptions of the 16 types in Chapter 2. Thank you also to Dr Jean Kummerow for permission to use her account of type development, updated in September 2011, which is featured on pages 119–28. Thank you to Esther Croom for her clear and quick work as the editorial assistant, and to Caroline Richards for her calm and skilful copy-editing and proofreading. And finally, thank you to Catherine Gray, my editor, for being supportive and challenging, and in particular for a moment in a conversation about the proposal for this book when I said, 'I want to write a magisterial book' (the word 'magisterial' took me by surprise but was exactly the right word). Catherine's instant reaction was that she didn't want a magisterial book and mine, at the same instant, was that I didn't want to write one either. And so it has proved!

Introduction

This book discusses how counsellors can use contemporary personality theory and research findings to improve their counselling. It reviews three major theories of personality and treats them as steps towards understanding people's individuality and not as labels or diagnoses which put people in rigid boxes. Rather, the ideas are used as anchors for an authentic sense of identity and as starting points for personality development, and the research findings are used as evidence for validity or as suggestions for new perspectives on clients' problems.

The three contemporary personality theories reviewed and applied to counselling in this book are:

1. McAdams' integrative model (chosen for its three domains – his carefully chosen term – of, broadly, preferences, motives and life stories).
2. Psychological type or preference theory (the most widely used approach in organisations for many years).
3. Five factor or 'Big Five' theory (the most prominent approach in the major personality journals for many years).

This choice of theories is not intended to disparage older theories; rather, it reflects the neglect in nearly all texts (Singer, 2005, is the only other exception I know of) of modern personality theory and research.

In Chapter 1, I argue that although there is strong evidence for counselling's effectiveness, there is also scope for improvement through using these three theories, particularly preference theory, and I discuss three areas of application: increasing self-awareness (of counsellors and clients), improving the counselling relationship, and clarifying clients' problems and their options for managing or resolving them. These applications and their potential for improving counselling's effectiveness are developed in the rest of the book.

Chapter 1

Personality and Counselling

This chapter discusses:

- the question 'What do we know when we know a person?', and Dan McAdams' answer to it of three domains, which are called in this book 'preferences', 'motives' and 'life stories';
- how personality defined in this way can be useful to counsellors: for increasing self-awareness, improving the counselling relationship and offering new perspectives on client problems;
- psychological type or preference theory and the concepts of preference and psychological type;
- the five factor or 'Big Five' theory of personality and reframing one of the factors, anxiety, as two preferences;
- personality development and change;
- using preference theory in counselling.

McADAMS' INTEGRATIVE MODEL OF PERSONALITY

Three fundamental questions about applying personality theories to counselling are how best to describe personality, how much it can change and what causes any changes. Dan McAdams answered the first question in particular in an article titled 'What do we know when we know a person?' (McAdams, 1995). In this article, which continues to be very influential among personality researchers, he described a conversation with his wife on the way home from a dinner party in which they talked about one of the guests, 'Lynn': their first impressions of Lynn, what they learnt about her, their feelings about her, their attempts to 'make sense of her'.

Counsellors also make sense of their clients and of themselves, and I will comment on the relevance of the McAdams' conversation about Lynn to counselling at several points in this summary of it. Of course, clients form impressions and make sense of their counsellors' personalities too – and I'll discuss some applications of personality to this aspect of counselling in Chapter 4 especially.

During their conversation, the McAdams sharpened, modified and organised their observations and impressions. And in his article and subsequent publications (e.g., McAdams & Pals, 2006; McAdams, 2009), Dan McAdams proposed that to understand a person requires at least three domains of knowledge about them, each of which is indispensable and incomplete in itself. In the rest of this section, I will illustrate these three domains with some examples of the evidence they collected and interpreted about Lynn's personality.

Dan McAdams' first impression of Lynn was that she was 'just too much', both physically and in the way she dominated the conversation. He described her as lively, sophisticated and articulate. His wife, who had a long one-to-one conversation with Lynn, agreed initially with him about her being 'too much' but then warmed to her, partly as a result of an intimate remark that suggested vulnerability. Lynn said: 'I've never believed in anything very strongly, nothing to get real passionate about. Neither did my parents, except for believing in us kids. They probably believed in us kids too much.'

Dan McAdams warmed to Lynn too, especially when she seemed genuinely interested in his work! Other evidence about her personality was that she talked loudly and quickly and held people's attention, that she had been married twice and her two children live with her first husband, that she was an atheist, drank more alcohol than most of the guests and hates jogging.

Domain one: traits (or preferences)

At this point McAdams phrased his initial question more precisely: 'But what is it that we thought we now knew about her? And what would we need to know to know her better?' (1995: 367–8). For him, the first domain is concepts which summarise characteristic patterns of thought and behaviour. For example, Lynn's behaviour suggested she was socially dominant, volatile and moody. McAdams uses the terms 'trait' and 'factor' to describe such patterns. I'll explain later in this chapter why I use the term 'preference', but the three concepts overlap in meaning and Lynn could with equal accuracy be described as (among other qualities) being extraverted (trait or factor) or as preferring Extraversion.

On a cautious note, the evidence about Lynn's traits or preferences was gathered on only one occasion, though in three situations – in a group and in one-to-one conversations with two different people. Ideally, for the most accurate impressions, Lynn would be observed in other settings and by more observers. However, this is rarely a practical option, and obviously not practical in one-to-one counselling, so it is fortunate that accurate impressions can be formed in one-to one-relationships (as discussed in Chapter 2).

Domain two: motives

The McAdams next discussed domain two of Lynn's personality, which Dan McAdams at different times has called 'personal concerns' and 'characteristic adaptations' and I call 'motives'. He describes this domain as 'vast and largely untapped' (1995: 376) and indeed it is something of a ragbag, including motives, interests, values, defence mechanisms, personal strivings, life tasks, conditional statements like 'Talks most when she's nervous', and many more frameworks and models. I think that the heart of domain two is assessing what a person wants and how she or he goes about achieving it (i.e., motives and associated behaviours).

Lynn said she was a pacifist and felt great compassion for the poor; an atheist but admired missionaries; had problems in intimate relationships; and wished she could believe in something. There are clues about motives, personal strivings and values in these statements, and in a counselling session these would probably become clearer more quickly than at a dinner party. Knowing Lynn's motives would be to know her more fully than only knowing her preferences, and, more importantly in counselling, help her to be clearer about these deeper aspects of herself.

Domain three: life stories

Domain three is about life stories and identity. A list of attributes from domains one and two is not an identity. Rather, McAdams is suggesting that Lynn would have constructed a story that links and makes sense of her past, present and future selves. It would be an evolving story or collection of stories and more difficult to gather information about in a relatively casual setting like a dinner party. Lynn's enigmatic remark about her lack of a passion and her parents' attitude is a clue, though. And is there a connection with her first husband's looking after their children? There are

Table 1.1 The variation of McAdams' model used in this book and related personality theories and concepts

Domain	Main related theories and concepts
1. Preferences	Preference theory, Big Five theory, preferences, traits, factors
2. Motives	Preference theory, motives, personal strivings, values, strengths
3. Life stories	Integrative life stories, scripts, archetypes

many possibilities e.g., a tragic story ('How I was ruined by my family'), an adventure story ('How I triumphed over adversity'), or an unfulfilled story ('How I'm searching for something to believe in').

Table 1.1 outlines the relationships between McAdams' domains and the other main personality theories and concepts used in this book.

In later chapters I will discuss applications of each of McAdams' three domains to counselling, treating domain one (preferences) as an outline of the person, though an outline which often provides valuable insights for counsellors and clients; domain two (motives) as adding depth and detail, useful for some clients and problems; and domain three (integrative life stories) as clarifying what a person's life overall means to them, and again useful for some clients and problems.

First, though, I'll review some of the research on the effectiveness of counselling and argue that applying McAdams' three domains can make it more effective. Three areas of application are emphasised: increasing self-awareness (developed particularly in Chapters 2, 3, 7 and 8), improving the counselling relationship (Chapter 4), and as a perspective on a wide range of clients' problems (Chapters 5 and 6).

You will find more about domain one (traits or preferences) in Chapter 2; domain two (motives) in Chapter 3; and domain three (life stories) in Chapter 8. McAdams' model of personality theory is valuable because of its range and depth. In my discussion of other personality theories which are in wide usage – namely, Big Five theory and psychological type theory – I will show how these three models complement each other.

HOW PERSONALITY THEORY IS IMPORTANT IN COUNSELLING

Research on the effectiveness of counselling

The evidence for counselling's effectiveness is now very strong (Wampold, 2007; Cooper, 2008; Duncan et al., 2010; Norcross & Wampold, 2011a,

2011b). However, this statement needs to be qualified in several respects: for example, these authors discuss how much effect counselling tends to have, how many hours of counselling are optimum, how long the effects tend to last, how effective it is compared to drug treatments and what it is about counselling that explains its success.

Counselling's effects are sometimes seen as modest, in line with Freud's remark about helping people change from 'neurotic misery' to 'common unhappiness'. On the one hand, this may sound realistic – counselling is not like reprogramming a computer or washing out a test tube; on the other hand, Mick Cooper and others see counselling as generally having a large effect. Thus, Cooper (2008: 22–3) characterised a typical effect as follows. A GP sees a patient, 'Frank', who has depression and he encourages Frank to wait and see how things go. The GP refers ten other patients who are about as depressed as Frank to a counsellor. Several well-designed studies suggest that after two months, about eight of the ten patients will feel significantly better than Frank and two will feel worse. On this view, counselling is considerably better than no treatment.

There is also recent strong research evidence on *how* counselling works. Elements of the counselling relationship such as empathy, collecting and using client feedback (Norcross & Wampold, 2011a) and collaboration (Tryon & Winograd, 2011) seem to be particularly important. For example, Tryon and Winograd (2011) carried out a meta-analysis of studies of collaboration and concluded that 'outcome appears to be considerably enhanced when patient and therapist are actively involved in a cooperative relationship' (2011: 50).

Matching characteristics of clients and aspects of counsellors and counselling is another strong possibility; for example, Norcross and Wampold concluded that 'different types of clients require different treatments and relationships' (2011b: 131). However, studying this idea is complicated because of the very large number of factors that could be influential – more than 200 have been suggested and at least 100 of these have been studied empirically.

Overall, counselling works and more is now known about how it works. However, there is still scope for improving its effectiveness and I discuss next some ways in which personality theory can contribute.

Increasing self-awareness

Self-awareness is a central concept in most if not all approaches to counselling and a prominent area of research in psychology (e.g., Vazire, 2010).

It can be defined as accurately knowing one's real feelings, wishes and thoughts. In a more abstract form, it is awareness of what Sidney Jourard (1971) called 'spontaneous inner experience', Abraham Maslow (e.g., 1968) the 'real self' and Carl Rogers (e.g., 1961) the 'organismic self'. In these phrases, the terms 'spontaneous', 'real' and 'organismic' rest on distinctions between being ourselves and living in line with the expectations of other people, and between authentic needs and inauthentic ones, even though false needs and false selves exist in their own right and therefore the term 'false' is a little clumsy.

This meaning of real self is elaborated on in Table 1.2. Elements of real selves as defined by Rogers and others are listed in the fluid inner sense of self-awareness and have obvious implications for counselling. The next sense – relatively stable inner self-awareness – raises two key questions for personality theory and for counselling: whether or not there are patterns in that fluidity and if so their nature. Finally, there is a third sense of self-awareness: impact on others through manner, appearance and actions, again with implications for counselling.

Table 1.2 A model of self and self-awareness

Kinds of self-awareness	Elements of self
More fluid inner self-awareness	Sensations
	Intuitions
	Thoughts
	Feelings
	Emotions
	Wishes
	Fantasies
	Wants/Intentions
More stable inner self-awareness	Preferences
	Traits
	Strengths
	Talents
	Values
	Attitudes
	Motives/Needs
	Memories
	Life stories
Outer self-awareness	Appearance
	Manner
	Actions

Source: Developed from Bayne et al. (2008: 163).

Many counsellors have experienced a client's relief and delight in discovering an aspect of their real self or understanding a problem in a new way because of that discovery. For example, consider a client ('Blossom') who was introduced to psychological type or preference theory, which is the theory used most in this book and represents domains one and two of McAdams' model.

> ### Blossom's preference for Introversion
>
> Blossom discovered that she was an introvert and that this was seen as OK by her counsellor. Before these discoveries, she had seen herself as a failed extravert, introversion as antisocial and extraversion as well adjusted. Blossom said: 'It's such a relief to learn that I'm not antisocial and that I don't have some deep personality defect – I just need more time to myself than some people and lots of peace and quiet!'
>
> Thus, Blossom became more accepting of an element of her real self and, more subtly, no longer criticised herself for not having the opposite quality, for being an unsuccessful extravert. And she went further. First, she identified three beliefs: that she was boring (because introverts are boring); that because she finds small talk 'excruciatingly tedious' people will give up on her and walk away; and that in order to be healthy and well balanced she'd have to change her personality, even though she didn't want to or know how to.
>
> Blossom challenged and replaced each of these beliefs and found that appreciating herself as an introvert also meant that she felt more confident socially: less worried about other people's reactions to her and more interested in how she felt in them. She took a further step: assertively expressing her needs by giving herself time to recover from periods of being sociable. Thus, at her brother's wedding, she escaped (her term) and read for an hour between dinner and dancing, enjoyed the social part more as a result, and explained to her brother what she was doing and why.

Overall, the assumption about self-awareness as a way of improving counselling's effectiveness is that increased awareness of one or more of one's preferences, motives and life stories will tend to improve decisions, relationships and feelings of well-being. Conversely, to the extent that people lack self-awareness – misjudge their personalities – they are more likely to miss opportunities, make costly errors and feel less happy and fulfilled.

Self-awareness in one or more of the three senses in Table 1.1 is of course also valuable, indeed vital, for counsellors themselves, personally and professionally. Professionally, it is central to several counselling qualities and skills: empathy requires counsellors to separate their own emotions from those of their clients, and maintaining boundaries depends on a counsellor's awareness of their reactions (an element of fluid inner self-awareness) as well as their ability to actually say 'no' with conviction or to make a request clearly (elements of outer self-awareness).

Improving the counselling relationship

Two of Bruce Wampold's conclusions from a review of research on the effectiveness of counselling were that clients' engagement in therapy is critical and that 'It appears that much of the variability among therapists is due to therapists' ability to form a working alliance with a variety of patients' (Wampold, 2007: 868). As touched on earlier, the related elements of a collaborative approach and matching clients and counsellors in various respects are also strongly supported as significant factors in explaining how counselling works and how it can be improved (e.g., Duncan et al., 2010; Norcross & Wampold, 2011a, 2011b).

Used well, personality theory can contribute to improving the counselling relationship. Awareness of personality differences increases the likelihood of accepting (in the core quality sense) and understanding people who are very different from ourselves, and of empathising with them more quickly and deeply. The alternative is judging some people who are different from ourselves as odd, difficult or even as having a personality disorder when, much of the time, they are just different and the difference is in a general sense desirable. This positive and constructive view of personality differences is a central theme in preference theory, which, in the form used in this book, proposes ten preferences and combinations of them. Thus, there is quite a lot of scope for both (unintentional) bias and greater acceptance and empathy.

More specifically, preference theory suggests the different 'languages' used by people with different combinations of preferences and how counsellors may therefore modify their own ways of communicating to match those of their clients, especially early in a counselling relationship. Most counsellors, and people in everyday life, adjust their communication style to other people's to some extent but can become more skilled by using a valid theory of personality differences. However, there is more to this aspect of matching than speaking the client's language, as discussed in Chapter 4. In addition, the theory suggests that some forms of counselling, some counsellors and some techniques suit clients with certain preferences more than those with the opposite preferences. And for counsellors, it suggests relationships between personality, choice of counselling orientation and feeling 'at home' with that orientation.

As a new perspective on client problems

Personality theory and research can provide useful perspectives on many problems with relationships, work, health and other aspects of life. For example, when one person in a couple is an introvert and the other an extravert, the introvert may wish to try sharing their thoughts, feelings and reactions more while the extravert might try being more sensitive to their partner's need for time alone.

The next sections of this chapter review and compare two further theories of personality: psychological type (also known as preference theory, based on the Myers-Briggs Type Indicator or MBTI) and five factor (or 'Big Five') theory. I'll discuss the concepts of preference and type, outline the standard eight preferences and five factors, and compare and critique the two theories on three criteria: validity, tone and versatility.

PSYCHOLOGICAL TYPE OR PREFERENCE THEORY

The concept of 'preference'

'Preference' can be defined as 'feeling most natural, energised and comfortable with particular ways of behaving and experiencing'. People generally behave in the ways they prefer, but can behave in the opposite way, though usually less frequently and with more effort. If you prefer introversion to extraversion, for example, then social events are likely to take more effort and energy than reading quietly and reflectively. However, most introverts can be sociable and most extraverts can reflect.

Moreover, introverts can understand extraversion intellectually but – according to preference theory – will never really know what it is like to actually be an extravert, or will know only in a pale, undeveloped form. For example, one of my students, who preferred extraversion, wrote: 'Whilst I feel expressive and articulate about the outside world I feel shy, awkward and inarticulate about my inner world. I would go so far as to say my inner world frightens me. It's like a bottomless pit that if I spend too much time exploring I might get lost in.'

I find this a very provocative comment because this student had good reflective skills, as shown in her writing and indeed in the quote itself, though she definitely did prefer extraversion. It goes to the heart of preference theory: each pair of preferences really is opposed and opposite and people thus are profoundly different in these respects. And when I consider my own preference for introversion by substituting 'inner' for 'outside' and 'outside' for 'inner', her remark makes more sense. I'd put it less strongly, perhaps because there is more pressure from society to develop extraversion than introversion, but I'm so much more at ease in my inner world. (Development of both preferences and non-preferences is discussed later in this chapter.)

'Preference' is very similar in form to the concept of 'strengths' as recently revived and refreshed by Alex Linley (2008). Indeed, preferences are broad strengths or sets of strengths in his use of the term. Linley's carefully expressed definition of a strength is 'a pre-existing capacity for a particular way of behaving, thinking, or feeling that is authentic and energising to the user, and enables optimal functioning, development and performance' (2008: 9).

Linley discusses each phrase in his definition (2008: 10–13), some key points for the concept of preference being:

- our strengths are inside us, either at birth or developed as children;
- when we use our strengths, we feel more real, fulfilled and energised;
- 'we learn better in the areas where we are already strong' (p. 13);
- doing something well isn't the same as enjoying it, though there is some overlap.

Preference is a broader concept than strength. Indeed, Linley proposes hundreds of strengths, whereas there are just eight preferences in standard psychological type theory. They are:

Extraversion (E) or Introversion (I)
Sensing (S)   or Intuition (N)
Thinking (T)   or Feeling (F)
Judging (J)   or Perceiving (P)

The meaning of each of the preferences is briefly indicated in Table 1.3 and is most clearly expressed as contrasts and matters of degree. Most people readily think of others who they can describe in part by one or more of the preferences, though usually using other terms – for example, practical versus dreamy for S and N, logical versus soft for T and F.

The phrase 'when developed' in the heading of Table 1.3 implies that the preferences are predispositions. In a good enough environment, they are expressed as characteristic experience and behaviour, and as they are

Table 1.3 Brief descriptions of the preferences (when developed)

E More outgoing and active	More reflective and reserved	I
S More practical, interested in facts and details	More interested in possibilities and an overview	N
T More logical and reasoned	More agreeable and appreciative	F
J More planning and coming to conclusions	More easy-going and flexible	P

expressed more they develop more. Thus, preference theory is optimistic: it assumes that most people's early socialisation encourages, or at least does not unduly discourage, development of their preferences.

For example, my father (who preferred Sensing and Thinking) had many practical skills and would have enjoyed introducing me (who prefers Intuition and Feeling) to carpentry, car maintenance and so on, and I asked my mother when I was an adult why he hadn't taught me about such things. She replied, 'You were always reading or playing football, dear.' If my father had tried, I would have learnt the skills but probably with an immense effort on both our parts and perhaps not very well. Development of Intuition (preference for N) tends to involve symbolic or abstract activities: psychology rather than surgery, advertising rather than accountancy.

Preference theory further assumes that people who do not express their preferences most of the time become 'frustrated, inferior copies of other people' (Myers with Myers, 1980: 189). A more gentle expression of this idea is that they feel less fulfilled and less effective than they would be as their real selves. Discovering your preferences, through counselling or other means, is usually reported to be like 'coming home', though it is sometimes more difficult to switch from non-preferences than it sounds (as discussed later in this chapter, in the section on personality change).

The concept of 'psychological type'

A person's 'type', as this term is used in current standard psychological type theory, includes one from each of the four pairs of preferences, for example ENTP or ESTJ. There are 16 such combinations and therefore 16 types.

The term 'type' can be a problem because it is readily associated with charlatans, mysticism and pseudo-science and because it is often dismissed as too simple and therefore insulting to individuality. My view is that it's dismissed too easily. First, there have consistently been prominent researchers who take it seriously (e.g., John & Robins, 1994; Dahlstrom, 1995; Vollrath & Torgersen, 2002; Haslam, 2007). Second, it can convey more information about a person's personality with greater economy than traits. For example, an animal can be described as quick, medium size and quite furry (traits) or a leopard (type).

This is not to say that people are types in the same way as animals are species; for a start, we are more able to pretend to have qualities which we don't have and more prone to self-deception. However, differences in personality are profound to the extent that the different types can seem like different species. As one of my students who preferred P (Perceiving – easy-going etc.) remarked after watching a group of people who prefer J (Judging – task-focused etc.) carry out an experiential exercise, 'I didn't know there were people like that!'

A third defence of the term 'type' in psychological type theory is that it doesn't mean 'This person is this type and therefore behaves only in these ways'. Rather, each type is defined as a set of preferences and therefore as tendencies to behave in certain ways but at the same time able to behave in the opposite ways. Preference theory states that most people, given normal development, behave consistently with their preferences most of the time and behave in ways associated with their non-preferences some of the time, and therefore can be predicted to a significant extent.

'Type' has another meaning in preference theory: type dynamics. This level of the theory suggests a personality structure for each psychological type and is regarded by most authoritative writers about type, for example in the MBTI Manual (Myers et al., 1998), as central. In marked contrast, some writers have recently argued that it is speculative at best and should be discarded or at least made less central (e.g., Lloyd, 2008; Reynierse, 2009, 2012), and I agree with them. I regard type dynamics, regretfully, as poorly supported empirically, and in this book I treat preferences as the main concept with type dynamics as an occasional source of ideas for strategies. (Type dynamics is illustrated in the first case study of type development in Chapter 7.)

In my view, Jim Reynierse has created a more useful meaning of 'type' than the standard one of ISTJ etc. He argued (Reynierse, 2012) that the best way to describe a person's personality is to put their preferences and non-preferences in rank order from most characteristic and developed to least. For example, a person's type could be PSTEIFNJ. A strength of this method is that the non-preferences become more explicitly and visibly acknowledged as part of each person's personality.

There will be more and richer descriptions or profiles too. Reynierse (2012) includes some brief examples but there are a lot of profiles to develop depending on which variation of his model is used. One variation is having different rank orders of the preferences to describe a person's personality in various situations. Just four situations, or kinds of situation, would mean 64 profiles. This I see as unnecessarily complicated because preferences transcend situations by definition; they are general characteristics. However, there is another level of preference theory, quite widely used, which suggests five facets for each preference (Quenk & Kummerow, 2011). This is called MBTI Step II and could eventually mean over a million profiles. Again, this seems too complicated for general use in counselling but does demolish criticisms of type theory as too crude and simple.

Returning to Reynierse's new meaning of type, he assumes that the most developed preference is opposed to the least developed one and so on. If that assumption is not made, then another variation with many more possible sequences and descriptions is created, for example SNPIFJTE with S the most developed preference, N the second and so on.

Three practical points for counsellors are worth emphasising at this point. First, each preference is useful on its own; preference theory has several levels. Second, an enormous number of profiles would be created by some of these variations but they still would not capture individuality in the same way that life stories do, nor would that be their purpose. Third, Reynierse uses MBTI scores to rank order each person's four preferences and four non-preferences, but although MBTI scores can be helpful they are not necessary (see Chapter 2). Preferences can be discovered using some of the other methods discussed in Chapter 2. Then, if desired, the question of which, if any, of your client's preferences and non-preferences are relevant to a particular problem can be explored, including if relevant which preference or non-preference is the most developed and which need developing further.

In the next two sections, I outline five factor theory and then compare it with preference theory in terms of validity, tone and versatility.

FIVE FACTOR THEORY OR THE 'BIG FIVE'

For many years, hundreds of personality characteristics were proposed and investigated and there were many attempts to bring order to them and find some consensus among theorists about which were the most important. Big Five theory was seen and continues to be seen by personality researchers as bringing that order, as a dramatic breakthrough (Funder, 2010). There are continuing problems with it, such as the best name for each characteristic,

Table 1.4 An indication of the meanings of the factors in Big Five theory

	High scorers	**Low scorers**
Extraversion	Adventurous	Withdrawn
	Outgoing	Reserved
Openness	Imaginative	Shallow
	Sophisticated	Unintelligent
Agreeableness	Soft-hearted	Cold
	Warm	Tough-minded
Conscientiousness	Organised	Careless
	Responsible	Weak-willed
Anxiety	Tense	Calm
	Anxious	Unemotional

its precise nature and whether there are other important personality differences, but these are all problems for preference theory too.

Probably the most widely used terms for the five factors are: extraversion, openness to experience, agreeableness, conscientiousness and neuroticism (anxiety). These categories, like the preferences, are very broad. Table 1.4 describes them briefly.

Reframing anxiety as two preferences

One of the advantages of Big Five theory over preference theory is that the latter does not have a characteristic that corresponds to low and high anxiety, and it would seem to detract from the largely positive tone of type profiles (see Tables 2.6 and 3.3). However, extensive research shows very clearly that anxiety is a major personality difference (e.g., Nettle, 2007; McAdams, 2009; Funder, 2010) and I argue that it can justly be treated as two preferences. I call these a preference for Calm (C) versus Worrying (W) and draw on Daniel Nettle's interpretation of theory and research that people who are low on anxiety have weaknesses and conversely that those who are highly anxious have strengths.

Most research on anxiety (and therefore on preferences for C and W) has concentrated – like much of psychology until positive psychology came to the fore in the last few years – on what were assumed to be clearly negative experiences and behaviours, for example, anxiety itself, depression, stress, conflict at work and home, and illness. For nearly all personality researchers, anxiety is a 'bad thing' (McAdams, 2006: 178). However, Nettle and others have drawn attention to associated strengths such as a tendency to persevere with difficult tasks (surprisingly perhaps) and to be prepared for problems (less surprisingly). People who prefer W (preference for Worrying) also tend to be more cautious and prone to rumination and obsessive behaviour – driven perhaps by fear of failure; however, in some activities rumination, in the sense of going over and over a set of details or a problem, helps to make success more likely. Clues for the preferences for C and W and further aspects of their meanings, including the strengths and weaknesses of preferring C, are discussed in Chapter 2.

COMPARING PREFERENCE THEORY AND THE BIG FIVE

Scores on the main questionnaires associated with these two theories correlate highly, for example, McCrae and Costa (1989) and Furnham (1996), and it is striking and dramatic that two theories developed in radically different ways (preference theory through clinical observation, Big Five theory through factor analysis) broadly agree on four of the five main personality characteristics. However, the two theories also differ significantly and in the next sections of this chapter I will compare them on the evidence for their validity, the tone of their descriptions of personality and their versatility.

Validity

Big Five theory has been investigated very extensively and rigorously (McAdams, 2009; Funder, 2010). The close relationship between the main measures of the preferences and the Big Five means that much of this research supports the validity of preference theory too.

An example of the validity research is the relationship between longevity and Conscientiousness (preference for Judging or Perceiving). Kern and Friedman (2008) combined data from 20 studies involving more than 8900 participants in several countries and found strong support for the finding that people high on Conscientiousness (with a preference for J) tended to live two to four years longer than people low on Conscientiousness (with a preference for P).

Those of us who prefer P (Perceiving) may be disturbed by this finding. However, it is a generalisation and in addition life seems to have become more complicated and unpredictable since these studies were carried out, thus possibly suiting those who prefer P more. On the other hand, this greater complexity seems more likely to reduce the longevity of people who prefer J (Judging) than to increase it for Ps. Not so cheerful! But as

Table 1.5 Personality and examples of consequential outcomes

Personality characteristic	Individual outcomes	Societal outcomes
EI	Happiness	Job satisfaction
SN	Drug misuse	Artistic interests
TF	Health	Job performance
JP	Longevity	Job performance
CW	Happiness	Job satisfaction

Source: Summarised from Ozer and Benet-Martinez (2006) and substituting the ten preferences for Big Five terms.

the reasons for the link between J and longevity become clearer they will probably suggest ways of helping everyone, regardless of personality, to live longer and well.

There are significant relationships between personality and many other important or 'consequential' outcomes, such as health, happiness, work performance and relationship success (Ozer & Benet-Martinez, 2006; Kuncel, Ones & Sackett, 2010), as summarised in Table 1.5. These effects are large in practical terms, comparable to those of socio-economic status and cognitive ability (Roberts et al., 2007; Kuncel, Ones & Sackett, 2010).

Tone

Tables 1.3 and 1.4 showed that the preference descriptions of personality are more positive than those of five factor theory. Table 1.6 shows that they are *much* more positive, though this statement needs to be qualified. First, a few five factor researchers have, somewhat grudgingly, made their descriptions a little less negative: for example, 'Easy going, not very well organised, and sometimes careless' for low Conscientiousness (the broad equivalent of preference for Perceiving) and 'You tend to express your anger directly' for low Agreeableness (preference for Thinking). However, negative terms (the writers would say 'accurate') are far more common in both the general and the research literatures of five factor theory. Second, preference theory does include a less glowing level of description but its initial and main emphasis is firmly on strengths.

McCrae and Costa (1989) concluded that personality descriptions based on the preferences were 'reasonably good' (in the sense of accurate) but that it may be better to reinterpret them in terms of their own (five factor) model, 'to include for example the antagonistic side of Thinking types and the lazy and disorganised side of Perceiving types' (1989: 36). However, my view is

Table 1.6 Comparing the tone of four of the preferences and the broadly equivalent factors: some examples

	Preferences	Big Five theory
Introversion (Low Extraversion)	Depth	Inhibited
Sensing (Low Openness)	Observant	Unimaginative
Thinking (Low Agreeableness)	Analytical	Unsympathetic
Perceiving (Low Conscientiousness)	Adaptable	Weak-willed

that just as, say, flexibility (part of the preference for P) taken to an extreme can be described as disorganised, so extreme conscientiousness (preference for J) can be described as rigid and obsessive. Overall, the emphasis on strengths in preference theory, with some attention to corresponding weaknesses, makes it more practical and appealing for counselling.

Preference theory is thus both more positive and more even-handed than Big Five theory in its descriptions of personality. This marked contrast is the result primarily of the difference between the concepts of preference and trait (or factor) as they are generally used. Preferences describe two opposite and equally positive qualities whereas traits treat each quality as something a person has more or less of, and one end of the dimension as better and healthier. John Lloyd expressed this contrast well in a detailed comparison of the two theories:

> If I discover I am an introvert, the Five-Factor model tells me I lack the much-to-be-desired trait of extraversion. Psychological Type tells me there are many advantages to being introverted, as well as areas of life where I may struggle. The Trait approach will leave me feeling a failure and inadequate; the Type approach will give me an affirming self-understanding that will help me. (Lloyd, 2012: 31)

Versatility

Preference theory is more versatile than five factor theory in several respects:

- It includes a model of normal development and ideas about obstacles to development and facilitating factors for it. It sees people as developing

both their preferences and their non-preferences (normally the preferences more). Five factor theory has little to say about personality development.
- It includes several levels of description (Bayne, 2005). Five factor theory has only two levels: the factors and 30 facets. However, there have recently been a few studies of combinations of two or three factors.
- It has been used in a much wider variety of settings so there is more experience to draw on for applications.

Overall, on these three criteria, preference theory is of equal value to or better than Big Five theory for use in counselling. Accordingly, I will use preference theory in most of the book, and ideas and findings from Big Five theory and research as a valuable supplement.

Counsellors are interested in personality development and change as well as increasing self-awareness and so on, and the next section reviews this aspect of preference theory in detail. I first touch on McAdams' domains, then illustrate development of the preferences and non-preferences through analysis of extracts from two of Carol Shields' novels. Next I briefly discuss personality change and then principles and strategies for developing the preferences.

PERSONALITY DEVELOPMENT

Each of McAdams' three domains has different implications for personality development, stability and change. Preferences (and traits) are relatively stable; motives, personal strivings and so forth are more likely to change over a lifetime and in different circumstances, though preference theory suggests that some motives are core and therefore, by definition, stable throughout life; and integrative life stories generally increase in unity and coherence with experience as we fashion and revise them, and can be radically changed.

Preference theory states that we develop both our preferences and our non-preferences throughout our lives. It assumes that most people develop their preferences first and most, and that this is natural and healthy. The descriptions of the preferences in Chapters 1, 2 and 3 assume normal development of preferences and non-preferences. For example, ENFPs (people who prefer Extraversion, Intuition, Feeling and Perceiving) tend to have such strengths as enthusiasm, liveliness and versatility, but also tend to have corresponding weaknesses such as trying to do too much, overlooking relevant details and not finishing projects. These weaknesses indicate relatively undeveloped S (Sensing) and J (Judging), two of ENFPs' non-preferences.

It is easy to think of environmental factors that can impede the development of a preference, such as a child who prefers T but is not allowed to argue, and one who prefers I but is not allowed time alone. Such factors discourage children from expressing their preferences and at the same time encourage them (probably with love and good intentions) to express and develop their non-preferences. In the theory, children are seen as needing people and activities which encourage or at least do not actively discourage expression, and therefore development, of their preferences. Their upbringing needs to be 'good enough'. The preferences are seen as quite resilient, but there may well be substantial individual differences in this resilience.

Carol Shields illustrated central aspects of development of the preferences vividly in the following extracts from her novel *The Box Garden* (1977) and a companion novel, *Small Ceremonies* (1976). In *The Box Garden* her character Charleen analyses the way Eugene always finds 'the most kindly interpretation' of other people's behaviour. This is a clue for a preference for F (preference for Feeling). Shields wrote:

> 'Kindness after all comes to him naturally; he was hatched in its lucky genre and embraces its attributes effortlessly. Gentleness, generosity and compromise are not for him learned skills: they have always been with him, wound up with the invisible genes which determine the wooliness of his hair and the slightly vacant look in his grey eyes .... He is not at the frontier as I am.' (1977: 104)

Charleen sees kindness and gentleness (which are central characteristics of a preference for F) as effortless and genuine for Eugene, in contrast to herself. She elaborates next on what it is like for her to be at the frontier of kindness. She thinks: 'For me kindness is an alien quality; and like a difficult French verb I must learn it slowly, painfully, and probably imperfectly ... it does *not* wake with me in the mornings; every day I have to coax it anew into existence, breathe on it to keep it alive, practice it to keep it in good working order' (1977: 104). She then adds that the most difficult aspect of all is appearing to be gentle and kind in a spontaneous and genuine way like 'true practitioners, its lucky heirs who acquire it without laborious seeking, the lucky ones like Eugene'. She thus, although very able intellectually, has laboured to appear F for many years (she is about 38 years old) and yet this aspect of F still doesn't feel natural.

Conversely, Charleen's preference for T (Thinking) does seem genuine, though there are no signs of her appreciating its strengths. Apart from her struggles with F, the evidence for Charleen's preference for T is the sustained analytical tone of her reflections and their content, and that in *Small Ceremonies*, Charleen's sister, who is a biographer with a 'delight in sorting out personalities', observes that Charleen, 'for all her sensitivity, has a core of detachment' (1976: 18).

Several aspects of preference theory are eloquently illustrated in these extracts: the centrality of effort versus naturalness in defining the idea of a preference, the pressure on women in Western culture to behave in F ways, the impact of this pressure on women's sense of self and self-esteem, the oppositeness of each pair of preferences, and the genetic component of personality. The latter is stated clearly but too strongly in her analysis, though this is a very complex subject (Pinker, 2002; Caspi, Roberts & Shiner, 2005; Rutter, 2006; Funder, 2010). Even a characteristic like woolly hair, which is probably strongly genetic and only influenced by one or a few genes, can be affected environmentally (by hair treatments, for example), while personality characteristics are probably affected by multiple genes, each having a small effect, and by many environmental factors.

PERSONALITY CHANGE

The preference theory view of change is illustrated by Carol Shields' character Charleen. The basic assumption in the theory is that preferences and non-preferences develop rather than change – and further, that this is desirable. The resulting stability underlies in part our sense of identity and gives meaning to our relationships. It means, if options are available, that we can choose friends, partners and work that suit us – which might mean that they share some or all of our preferences or that we, deliberately or unknowingly, are drawn to a person or activity which brings out our non-preferences. Either way, some stability of personality is essential and our lives would be very different without it.

The preferences can act as an 'anchor' for our sense of self. However, as people get older, and perhaps most often in middle age, some of us become very interested in developing our non-preferences more. The idea of preferences also implies realistic expectations of the limits of personality change through counselling: for example, someone who, like Charleen, develops her F (Feeling) through intensive practice, still prefers T (Thinking). Even theorists who argue for a fluid, constructivist approach to personality probably assume some stability of personality when choosing partners, friends and colleagues. It follows too that it is helpful for counsellors and clients to accept that there are limits on changing some aspects of personality.

An apparent exception

Myers with Myers (1980) refer to 'falsification of type', a process 'which robs its victims of their real selves and makes them into inferior, frustrated copies of other people' (1980: 189). Thus, when someone has developed their non-preferences most they tend, according to the theory, not to feel right. If they then, probably through a friendship, romantic relationship or counselling, begin to express their true preferences more, personality 'change' can be very sudden and dramatic.

However, for some people the change from a false self to expressing their preferences is more of a struggle. For example, one of my students wrote in her journal about the impact of discovering her preference for P (Perceiving): 'I know now I am a P ... my view of tasks is becoming more P and I'm actually getting more done', but where some people find such a change easily liberating and fulfilling, Helen felt her preference for P and non-preference for J to be 'at war', although still with a sense of progress (Bayne, 2005: 62). The crucial factor may be that Helen had *behaved* in a J way for many years rather than just seeing herself as J but actually behaving P. In contrast, the two examples of apparent change of type discussed early in Chapter 2 are changes of perception more than behaviour, as is the example of Blossom earlier in this chapter.

A complication here is the difference between falsification of type and development of a non-preference. I see falsification as behaving primarily and for a long period in ways that express a non-preference. There is also an implication that the person has never been aware – or at least not clearly aware – of this self-alienation, or has gradually lost that awareness. On the positive side, they will have developed their non-preference, perhaps to its limit for them, through intensive, though unfulfilling, practice.

A formal and valid measure of preference development is not available yet (Bayne, 2005) but might in any case not be practical for most counsellors and clients. It is likely to be elaborate and will require specialist training; it might also threaten the collaborative, non-judgemental nature of the good counselling relationship.

DEVELOPING THE TEN PREFERENCES

Four general principles

Use these principles to develop preferences:

1. Recognise the difference between developing a skill associated with a preference, on the one hand, and on the other, developing the preference itself in a way that involves what Katherine Myers and Linda Kirby call 'truly understanding' it (1994: 32). I don't know of any research on this distinction. I suspect that most of us develop our non-preferences in a patchy way and that we don't understand them in the way we do our preferences.
2. See the positive aspects of all the preferences. The most problematic in this respect is probably W (preference for Worrying), though all the preferences have been evaluated negatively at times, as illustrated in Table 4.1 in Chapter 4.
3. Compare your attempts to develop a non-preference with someone for whom it is a well-developed preference. This can be very salutary.
4. Practise hard, but check your reaction often and be ready to stop. Keep going only while it's still enjoyable (easier for Ps). In other words, 'Don't be too ambitious' (Myers, K. & Kirby, 1994: 33).

This fourth principle is necessarily vague; like much of counselling, it is a matter of supporting and challenging with good timing. It also goes against the recently popularised idea – by Malcolm Gladwell and others, based on research by Ericsson in particular – that 10,000 hours of intensive practice is needed to develop excellence (e.g., Ericsson, Krampe & Tesch-Roemer, 1993). Willingham (2007) cites studies of numerous kinds of expertise, including musical composition and performance, tennis and livestock evaluation, to support this view, calling it the 'ten year rule' (2007: 400).

Preference theory suggests ceiling effects, that is, a maximum capacity set by genes, and that intensive practice without genetic talent is not enough. It is not possible for anyone to be anything they wish. Moreover, talent in the form of strong motivation seems likely to be necessary to *sustain* the intensive practice; for example, being generally kind and gentle comes easily in part because of a preference for F.

Indeed, Ericsson defined effective practice as having the following characteristics, with the first undermining his position that talent isn't a useful concept:

- The person must be motivated.
- The task must be at the appropriate level: neither too easy, so that the person can perform it effortlessly, nor too difficult, so that the person cannot perform it.
- There must be immediate corrective feedback.
- It involves the repetition of the same or similar tasks. (Willingham, 2007: 445)

There are two caveats to the principles above. The first, from Isabel Myers, is that however well developed our preferences and non-preferences are, she, like Jung, saw everyone as having a 'shadow side' (1980: 84). I interpret Myers' use of 'shadow' here not in the sense of a dynamic unconscious (Smith et al., 2012) but as the non-preferences being less developed than the preferences and therefore less mature and potentially troublesome. However, the more psychodynamic emphasis does exist in the preference theory literature, for example, Naomi Quenk's ideas about stress and being 'in the grip' (Quenk, 1996, 2002).

The second caveat is that more complex approaches to developing the preferences are prominent in this literature. They either emphasis type dynamics or what are called 'function attitudes', or both. In the function attitudes model, the preferences for S, N, T and F each have an introverted and an extraverted variation (Thompson, 1996; Hartzler & Hartzler, 2005). Many MBTI practitioners see the shadow side, type dynamics and function attitudes as very powerful (and they are illustrated in the first long case study in Chapter 7), but until better evidence is available for them I'll use the simpler preference level of the theory in this book.

Strategies

Often the same activity can be done with different preferences. For example, you can cook, garden or play chess (in very different styles) using any of the preferences. Some of the strategies for developing the preferences listed in Table 1.7 therefore need to be made more specific by each counsellor and client. Similarly, as implied earlier in defining 'preference', perhaps try a strategy for five minutes or so the first time and see how natural or strained it feels. If it does feel natural, even slightly, then it's probably working.

Table 1.7 Strategies for developing preferences

For Extraversion	• Be spontaneous • Speak to an audience • Speak to someone you don't know
For Introversion	• Be alone for longer than usual for you • Listen when you want to speak • Read quietly for longer than usual for you
For Sensing	• Observe and keep observing (an exercise prominent in mindfulness) • Be very specific about something • Focus on someone's actual words and how they speak, including gestures and changes in tone
For Intuition	• Brainstorm • Give an overview • Focus on possible underlying meanings of what someone is saying and not saying
For Thinking	• Create a flow chart • Do a cost–benefit analysis for a decision • Define something precisely
For Feeling	• Clarify your values • Give a compliment • Reflect on what matters most to someone you know well
For Judging	• Make a list of things to do • Do them and tick each one off as you finish • Resist an impulse which you'd normally act on
For Perceiving	• Act on an impulse • Re-examine a decision and gather more information • Relax instead of completing or finishing something
For Calm	• Do relaxation exercises • Avoid caffeine and other stimulants • Practise mindfulness
For Worrying	• Reflect on all the possible negative results of an action • Try to feel an emotion more intensely than you usually do • Prepare carefully for a problem which may arise

AN OVERVIEW OF HOW COUNSELLORS CAN USE PREFERENCE THEORY

Some counsellors use preference theory like any other framework (e.g., loss or assertiveness), when it seems appropriate for a particular client. For example, you may think of it only when a client communicates in a way you find difficult and then just one or two of the preferences may be relevant. Other counsellors use the theory more as an intrinsic part of their model of counselling, and in a variety of ways as their knowledge and experience develops, while a few routinely ask their clients to complete the MBTI before starting counselling and then begin the first session with a discussion of the results. Indeed, one said to me that he wouldn't counsel somebody without doing this.

However, using preference theory without the MBTI is emphasised in this book, because it is often more practical and more desirable not to use it in counselling and because using it requires specialised training. 'Many therapists use type concepts without administering the actual MBTI to clients' (Provost, 1993: 26).

CONCLUSIONS

1. The three domains of preferences, motives and life stories bring some clarity and order to the concept of personality.
2. Some of the main factors influencing the effectiveness of counselling are the core qualities of empathy and acceptance, a collaborative approach including taking client feedback seriously, and aspects of matching counsellors and clients.
3. Counselling can become more effective still by applying personality theory and research to these factors and in three broad areas: self-awareness, the counselling relationship and client problems.
4. Traits and preferences are real and significant influences on experience and behaviour.
5. How counsellors can use preference theory (in its MBTI or Myers-Briggs Type Indicator sense) will be the main focus of this book, with ideas and findings from Big Five theory a valuable supplement.
6. Anxiety (Neuroticism) from Big Five theory will be treated as two new preferences, for Calm versus Worrying.
7. With some clients, none of the preferences will be relevant; with others, one preference may be useful, and so on through several degrees of increasing complexity.
8. How developed a client's preferences and non-preferences are, and might usefully become, is a further level of application.
9. Contemporary personality theory illuminates and potentially improves counselling in many respects but there is still much that is mysterious about both personality and counselling.

APPENDIX: SUMMARY OF SINGLE-LETTER ABBREVIATIONS FOR THE TEN PREFERENCES

The summary letters for the ten preferences used in this book are listed below. Please note that the terms are technical ones – they have their own meanings which are not the same as their everyday meanings. Their meanings in the theory were indicated in Tables 1.3 and 1.4 and are discussed in more detail in Chapter 2.

E   Extraversion
I   Introversion
S   Sensing
N   Intuition
T   Thinking
F   Feeling
J   Judging
P   Perceiving
C   Calm
W Worrying

In the rest of this book, I will generally refer to each preference with a single letter, as in 'Es tend to talk more loudly'. This is shorthand for:

> People with a preference for Extraversion tend to talk more loudly than people with a preference for Introversion, but can on occasion talk more softly too, depending on other factors such as their sensitivity to the particular situation, their assessment of it and how much they have developed this element of their Introversion (their non-preference). Moreover, there are some (a few) people with a preference for Introversion who habitually talk loudly, perhaps because they grew up in a large family or for some other reason.

Chapter 2

Increasing Self-awareness 1: Discovering the Preferences

This chapter discusses:

- four general principles for discovering the preferences;
- two examples of people who found discovering one or more of their preferences difficult;
- a choice of strategies for helping your clients discover their preferences during a counselling session;
- two extra strategies for outside a counselling session;
- questions clients may ask about the preferences.

Some aspects of the principles and strategies for discovering a person's preferences described in this chapter will come easily to many counsellors: in particular, they involve listening sensitively and accepting differences in personality, values etc. between you and your client. What may come less easily is what Sally Carr (1997: 1) called 'detective work': looking for clues for each preference and helping your client weigh the evidence.

Carr usefully defined what she called 'clarifying preferences' as 'a sifting process, in which the practitioner tries to help the client to isolate their basic, enduring preferences from other influences on their behaviour' (1997: 2). Given that the 'other influences' include situations, upbringing, motives, roles, stress and other personality characteristics, this can be a formidable task, but it is feasible (Funder, 2010; Vazire, 2010; Beer & Brooks, 2011). Indeed, people generally observe traits – and therefore preferences – quite accurately, but there is scope for improvement and most of us can remember vivid first impressions of personality which were wrong – by us of others and by others of us!

The very brief descriptions in Chapter 1 of characteristics associated with the ten preferences (eight from standard MBTI theory plus Calm versus Worrying) allow their observation in oneself and others. Please treat any such judgements, and judgements based on the strategies and more detailed descriptions in this chapter, as *provisional*.

FOUR GENERAL PRINCIPLES FOR DISCOVERING THE PREFERENCES

These are the four principles:

1. *Resist any pressure to decide quickly.*

   Rather, 'set the scene for the search' (Myers & McCaulley, 1985: 57). It's not a bad thing to be unclear: a preference may not apply to a particular person, and people's personalities are much more complex than any theory.

2. *Remember that it is the person who decides what their preferences are (or indeed if they have preferences at all).*

   This is also a general principle of some approaches to counselling. For example, Mearns and Thorne wrote that 'the counsellor's understanding is not the aim … the aim is to create the conditions where the client comes to understand himself' (2007: 83). Jung was also clear on this: 'It is relatively unimportant whether the psychotherapist understands or not, but everything hangs on the patient's doing so' (source unknown).

3. *Look for the best fit, not a perfect fit.*

   This principle follows directly from the concept of preference. We have all developed our preferences and non-preferences to varying degrees and many of us have learned some patterns of behaviour which express our non-preferences. This fact also makes accurate observation of our true preferences more difficult.

   When someone is puzzled about a preference, it can often be explained by one facet of a preference being inconsistent (in terms of preference theory) with the others. For example, talking freely about oneself is a good clue for a preference for E (Extraversion) but some Introverts talk freely too (Quenk & Kummerow, 2011). Their preference, though, is still for Introversion and 'Introverted' is still a useful way of describing their personality, both for self-understanding and for predicting their behaviour.

4. *Behave like a good detective.*
   - Look for clues – pieces of evidence – both for and against each preference. In particular, treat early impressions as hypotheses and beware of the disproportionate power of first impressions.
   - Look for *why* people do things (e.g., motives and values – discussed in Chapter 3).
   - Think of alternative explanations for clues: for example, some situations tend to constrain behaviour more than others. A useful precaution is to try to distinguish between a judgement and the evidence it is based on.
   - Accept that 'There are no infallible indicators of personality. There are only clues and clues are always ambiguous' (Funder, 2010: 57).

TWO CASE STUDIES

These two brief case studies are examples of correcting initial misjudgements of preferences made by the person themselves. Both completed the MBTI, which is on average about 75% accurate (Myers et al., 1998: 116). However, as touched on at the end of Chapter 1 and discussed later in this chapter, this isn't a necessary part of discovering one's preferences (though it is often a valuable starting point).

The first case study is of Sally Carr. Her MBTI results were ENTP (preferences for Extraversion, Intuition, Thinking and Perceiving – see Table 1.1 and the detailed analyses in this chapter), and she commented that she found this a 'reasonable enough fit. However, it never seemed to do anything for me or help me to understand my reactions' (1997: 20). This is not the usual or desired outcome of discovering your preferences!

In particular, Sally struggled with S (preference for Sensing) versus N (Intuition). On the one hand, she was academically successful in an abstract discipline (psychology). On the other hand, she discovered that she believed she *should* prefer N ('shoulds', of course, often being a warning signal). Moreover, she realised that she focused easily on practical things and that her main approach to understanding theories was through specific examples. A preference for S was beginning to look more likely, so she tried a week's experimenting with behaving like an ESTP and felt liberated by both the prospect and the experience.

I discovered my own preferences in another way. My MBTI results were INTJ and Jan (preferences for ISTJ), who knew me well, said they were wrong and that I was an INFP. My view was that she was a very clear TJ and that I was a less clear TJ but still a TJ, and I left it there for over a year. This error (as it turned out to be) is partly explained by my being so pleased with the IN part of my result that I took it for granted that the TJ part was accurate too. I also liked the INTJ profile most! During the year, I tried out INFJ in a rather desultory and casual way (another clue) before realising that I am an INFP.

Thus, perceptive friends can be good sources of evidence, especially if listened to seriously. When I look at colleagues who are INTJs (there is a high proportion of INTJs in academic life; much lower in counselling) I wonder how I could ever have thought Jan was wrong.

STRATEGIES FOR HELPING CLIENTS DISCOVER THEIR PREFERENCES IN A COUNSELLING SESSION

Observations of a client's preferences (and of other aspects of their personality) can be made either implicitly or collaboratively, or implicitly first and collaboratively later. An example of an implicit observation is that a client seems to the counsellor to be quiet and reflective, and the counsellor adjusts his characteristic fast pace accordingly without saying anything about his observation or the consequent change to his client. Such adjustments are also often made naturally in everyday conversations. Later, this counsellor and client may discuss the counsellor's judgement and change of pace, especially if it seems relevant to their therapeutic relationship or to a problem the client has raised.

A more complex example of implicit assessment is that you observe that your client (X) is not using emotion words and so consider several possible explanations:

- X does not trust you at this point;
- X is not aware of her emotions;
- X seems to have few words for emotions;
- X may prefer T (Thinking) and be talking in the language she's most comfortable with (how aware or not she is of her emotions cannot be accurately observed yet);

■ X may prefer F (Feeling) but has developed her non-preference for T more.

You may choose in this situation to keep your observation implicit, at least for a while and to see if any of the explanations can be eliminated or can become the 'prime suspect'. In terms of your behaviour, you may decide not to use emotion words yourself – or perhaps one or two relatively straightforward ones with particular care and gentleness – and not to persist if the client ignores them, thus showing acceptance of your client's way of speaking at this time.

A further alternative is to say to your client, 'I notice that you like to analyse and that you haven't talked about your feelings …'. This riskier option could be the beginning of a collaborative approach to assessing aspects of your client's personality. A further possibility is that your client asks you directly to help them work on their self-awareness, decide what careers would suit them better, improve a relationship, feel more fulfilled, and so on. In each of these circumstances, you might suggest ways of helping them discover their preferences, motives or life stories.

Discovering your own or a client's preferences is, in my experience, likely to happen more quickly through using one or more of the following strategies than it did in the two examples described in the previous section of this chapter.

Be clear about the meaning of each preference

In part, this means emphasising the comfort and energy central to 'preference' (as discussed in Chapter 1). A potential difficulty is that the terms for the preferences and the Big Five factors are open to misinterpretation; however, they usually make enough initial sense to be useful quite readily. Another (minor) complication is that occasionally activities associated with a person's preferences are spoken about in a taken-for-granted way rather than with energy and pleasure.

Later in this chapter I have listed the clues for each preference which I see as most observable in counselling and most valid. I've used a wide range of sources, from expert opinion to sophisticated empirical research but the clues do have limitations: the effects of culture, age and other factors on whether and how preferences are expressed, disputes about the central defining qualities of each preference, and the small relationships between clues and preferences (hence looking for patterns and behaving like a good detective).

Moreover, expert observers sometimes disagree radically. For example, here are two views on making lists as a clue for J versus P. First, Wennik (1999) wrote that people who prefer Judging 'are the list makers' and that 'It doesn't make sense to Perceivers to make lists, since they aren't going to stick to them anyway. Lists and plans are just too stifling' (1999: 41). Wennik therefore sees making lists as differentiating very clearly between Js and Ps and also speculates in dramatic terms about the related motives. Second, Murray (1995) wrote that Js make lists, usually written down and 'in priority order' and that Js also 'do the items on the list usually in the order planned'. However, he disagreed with Wennik about Ps and lists: in his view Ps make lists too but are 'more casual' about them (1995: 102).

I agree with Murray that both Js and Ps make lists (I think it's far more common to make lists than not to), but that Ps are less likely to act on their lists or to tick off the items, and more likely to lose them. Moreover, I suspect a radical difference in reasons for making lists: that Js' lists are primarily for action and Ps' lists are for increasing their sense of what there is to do when and if they feel like doing it. However, no one has yet actually reported a study of personality and making lists and treatment of the lists, so our three views are all just opinions.

Much stronger evidence than expert opinion on useful clues for clarifying the preferences is provided by recent studies using Electronically Activated Recorders (EAR) and Daily Diary Completions. Both these methods focus in detail on what people actually do in their daily lives. For example, the EAR is a pocket-sized digital audio recorder with a microphone which can be attached to a collar. It records (say) for 30 seconds four times an hour and participants don't know when it's recording – they do, though, have an opportunity to listen to the recordings and edit them before giving them to the researcher, but in practice rarely change them (Mehl et al., 2006).

A meta-analysis of research on how traits (and this research is equally about preferences, as discussed in the section on validity in Chapter 1) are expressed in behaviour used an electronic device to remind participants to report on their behaviour every two to four hours during the day for one to two weeks. Twenty thousand reports were produced altogether (Fleeson & Gallagher, 2009). The authors describe the results as 'surprisingly strong' (2009: 1107): they found that traits (and therefore preferences) are 'powerful predictors' of everyday behaviour.

However, and in line with the concept of preference, Fleeson and Gallagher also found that the range of behaviour in each person is quite diverse and that what traits predict is *average* behaviour. For example, 'extraverts quite regularly act introverted and introverts quite regularly act extraverted', and people very low on Agreeableness (who prefer Thinking) are 'quite friendly and polite most of the time' but 'a little less warm a little more often' (2009: 110).

These differences may sound small but they matter: people are far from interchangeable in personality. However, the overlaps in the behaviour of people with opposite preferences clearly make accurate discovery of preferences more difficult. A second implication is that general clues, summarising clusters of relatively specific behaviours, are the most likely to be valid – for example, a term and clue like 'warm'.

To make accurate judgements of a personality characteristic, three elements are needed. First, clues which are relevant to the particular characteristic and which can be observed. Second, actually observing those clues. And third, making the connections between clues and characteristic (Funder, 2010; Beer & Brooks, 2011). The clues can come from observation of behaviour or from reports by the person or people who know them. Errors are possible at each stage. Not surprisingly, personal information is a positive factor (Beer & Brooks, 2011) and counsellors are in a good, indeed privileged, position in this respect.

Clues for Extraversion (E) versus Introversion (I)   Table 2.1 shows some characteristics associated with preferences for Extraversion and Introversion.

Introverts need to be alone more than Extraverts, partly to recover from social contact and restore inner harmony, partly because Is tend to be more interested in their own thoughts and reactions than in what is going on.

Many Introverts enjoy socialising, even sometimes in large groups, but find it depleting. So you may meet someone who is bubbly and socially skilled and an Introvert. Conversely, there are people who can accurately be described as shy Extraverts.

Table 2.1   Some characteristics associated with preferences for E and I

Extraversion	**Introversion**
Prefer the outer world of people and things to reflection	Prefer reflection and the inner world
More active and adventurous	More reserved and cautious
Gain energy more from others, need less time alone	May enjoy social contact but need more time to recover
Like variety and versatility more	Like depth and specialism more

Despite these and other complications, answers to the following questions can give useful clues to preference for E versus I. At a party (if you go to parties), are you more likely to circulate happily or to talk to one or two people? What are you more likely to do to recover when you're stressed or drained: seek others out or retreat to a quiet place? And how do you generally prepare for a meeting or activity – by talking or withdrawing?

Susan Brock (1994) recommended speech characteristics as particularly useful clues for E and I: in her experience, Es tend to speak more quickly and loudly, to interrupt and to think out loud. They tend to direct their energy outwards. Mehl et al. (2006) found that Es tend to talk more, to talk more about themselves and to spend less time alone.

A possible core quality of E is positive emotions. Indeed, some researchers have gone so far as to suggest renaming E as Positive Emotionality because the relationship is so clear. Matthews et al. (2009) criticise this view strongly but Nettle (2007) sees positive emotion as the key to E, arguing that joy, enthusiasm etc. are all in response to 'the pursuit or capture of some resource that is valid' (2007: 85). By 'resource' he means new friendships, higher status and new skills or challenges – all in the outside world.

Introverts take a more measured approach to such resources but it is not necessarily an unhappy one – rather, material possessions, relationships etc. have less effect. Nor is it necessarily a disadvantage: 'The introvert is, in a way, aloof from the rewards of the world, which gives him tremendous strength and independence from them' (Nettle, 2007: 92).

Clues for Sensing (S) versus Intuition (N)   Table 2.2 shows some characteristics associated with preferences for Sensing and Intuition.

People who prefer S tend to be more observant than Ns and thus to be more precise and detailed when describing something or someone or giving directions. People who prefer N tend to talk more generally ('It's

Table 2.2   Some characteristics associated with preferences for S and N

Sensing	Intuition
More realistic and practical	More imaginative and speculative
More observant about what is actually happening	More likely to see the 'big picture'
More drawn to details generally	Less patient with details generally
More patient with routine and things as they are	More drawn to variety, more easily bored, more unconventional

Table 2.3 Some characteristics associated with preferences for T and F

Thinking	Feeling
More analytical and logical	More warm and sympathetic
More brief and business-like	More focused on how they and other people are feeling
More critical (with the intention of improving whatever is criticised)	Greater need for harmony
More sceptical and tough minded	Enjoy pleasing others more

NB: Ts have emotions, Fs can be logical.

over there'), to give overviews and be more interested in links and possibilities than in what is actually there.

Clues for Thinking (T) versus Feeling (F)   Table 2.3 shows some characteristics associated with preferences for Thinking and Feeling.

People who prefer T tend to be more interested in ideas and reasons than in emotions. Thus they are more likely to enjoy debating issues than they are to express enthusiasm or revulsion about them. They are also more able to detach themselves from a situation while Fs more readily place themselves in it and see other people's points of view. Similarly, Ts suppress their emotions more often in order to keep their minds clear while Fs' emotions are generally central for them and vital in making decisions. Thinking is detached and logical while Feeling is subjective and evaluative.

A related characteristic is that Fs are more likely to offer praise and appreciation and Ts to criticise. They do not usually mean the criticisms personally; indeed, their aim is a constructive one and it is a compliment that they consider it worthwhile to help. However, Fs may not see it in the same way, even after knowing about preference theory! Similarly, Fs tend to have a more trusting view of others (in the extreme, to be gullible or submissive), while Ts tend to be more sceptical (in the extreme, harsh or even cruel). People who prefer Feeling 'Tend to express sympathy and warmth and are generally unconfrontational' (Mehl et al., 2006: 867). Gender is another clue to T and F since general population surveys in the USA and UK suggest that about 60% of men prefer T and about 60% of women prefer F.

Clues for Judging (J) versus Perceiving (P)   Table 2.4 shows some characteristics associated with preferences for Judging and Perceiving.

People who prefer J tend to particularly enjoy making decisions and finishing things. They are usually task-focused and believe that work

Table 2.4 Some characteristics associated with preferences for J and P

Judging	Perceiving
More decisive	More curious
More organised and systematic	More flexible and easy-going
Tend to start projects well before deadlines to avoid last-minute pressures	Tend to have a last-minute imminent deadline energy surge and to enjoy it
Tend to value plans more	Tend to see how things go

NB: Judging does not mean judgemental.

comes before play. They therefore tend to be more serious and formal whereas people who prefer P tend to be more easy-going and flexible, believing that as far as possible work and play are the same and that it's best to see what will happen, to go with the flow.

Thus, Js plan and Ps adapt. Js want most to achieve the outcome, Ps to look for ways to enrich it but also with the attitude 'What if I don't want to do what we've planned when the time comes?'. It follows that self-discipline is more natural for Js, low impulse control more natural for Ps. When cooking, Js may clear up as they go along, Ps create apparent chaos then swiftly clear up at the end. When challenged, they might say, 'How can you stop the flow?'

Another good clue for identifying J and P is response to deadlines. Most Ps find that they have an imminent deadline energy surge – that they do their best work, gain focus and energy, at the last minute. In contrast, most Js start early – they find deadlines more stressful than stimulating. Js' greater enjoyment of closure may also be a factor. Ps like to keep things open, especially if they prefer E and N as well.

Keith Richards gave a good illustration of J versus P in an interview quoted by Sean O'Hagan (*The Observer*, 25 April 2010). Richards said that 'Mick needs to know what he's going to do tomorrow. Me, I'm just happy to wake up and see who's hanging around. Mick's rock, I'm roll.'

Clues for Calm (C) versus Worrying (W)   Table 2.5 shows some characteristics associated with preferences for Calm and Worrying.

People who prefer Calm tend to approach life nonchalantly and optimistically, to be more resilient and emotionally stable and to cope relatively well with stress. Those who prefer Worrying tend to anticipate potential problems, be more volatile emotionally, feel more intensely and be more easily upset.

Table 2.5 Some characteristics associated with preferences for C and W

Calm	Worrying
More carefree and optimistic	More sensitive to potential risks
Less likely to experience 'negative' emotions like anxiety and sadness	More likely to get stressed about things they know are small or 'silly'
Less likely to complain	Slightly more likely to achieve 'success'
Quicker to recover from upset or loss	Slower to recover

People who prefer W tend to experience 'negative' emotions like fear, anxiety, sadness and disgust more than those who prefer C. Nettle argues that these emotions are helpful in detecting and avoiding potential dangers. For example, disgust helps Ws keep away from unhygienic or infectious situations. And sadness can be seen positively as 'a kind of energy-saving withdrawal from a plan that has failed' (2007: 109), or as a productive time to reflect on a mistake.

Nettle compares the role of negative emotions with that of smoke detectors. False alarms from smoke detectors are irritating but failures can be catastrophic. Therefore, smoke detectors tend to be set so that they're likely to give false alarms but very unlikely to fail when there's a real fire. People who prefer W are designed, in the evolutionary sense, to be hypersensitive for the same reason; 'Far better a little groundless worry than getting eaten or starving' (2007: 110).

People who prefer C are more likely to take risks, for example choosing activities and work like mountain climbing (E is a factor here too), police and the military which have relatively high mortality rates (Nettle, 2007). People who prefer W are at greater risk of clinical levels of depression and anxiety, though there are arguments for depression having a 'bright side' (Bugental & Bugental, 1980; Andrews & Thomson, 2009), in particular giving space and time for solving complex personal problems. The implication for treatment is obvious: to help depressed clients identify and solve such problems.

Preferring W is also related to being a writer, poet or artist. Nettle suggests several motives including self-therapy and wanting to improve the world because, he suggests, Ws don't feel right in the world the way it is. A preference for W is also associated with working very hard, which in turn is a factor in achieving success as generally defined. And Nettle suggests that business and politics would benefit from more people who have developed their W qualities, and that leaders tend to be too optimistic, too C. Optimism is a positive quality sometimes but often would benefit from being balanced by concern about possible negative consequences and threats.

I think Elaine Aron's extensive work (e.g., Aron, 1996, 2010) on the 'Highly Sensitive Person' is very relevant to the preference for W and indirectly for C as well. Unfortunately, she uses the abbreviation HSP for Highly Sensitive Person, which clashes with S and P in preference theory, but I'll only use HSP in this section.

There are several links between HSPs and preference for W. Aron sees HSPs as specialists in deep, careful observing – 'mindful' in the current sense of that term. HSPs notice more and consider consequences more before acting in new situations. Effects of this include being startled more easily, feeling more deeply – both positive and negative emotions – and getting tired more quickly because there is so much to observe and HSPs' reactions are so intense.

Aron's research also shows that HSPs are unusually creative, intuitive – getting a sense of trouble before it happens and making unexpected links – and compassionate. They have a strong aesthetic sense – for example, enjoying making what to most people would be small changes to enhance their homes. At the same time they tend to lose confidence relatively easily and feel overwhelmed. And others readily accuse them of being 'fusspots', and of taking things too personally or too seriously.

A vital concept for understanding HSPs is fit with their environment. Indeed, there is a parallel here with the other eight preferences and their development: we all benefit from finding or creating environments that encourage (or at least allow) us to express our preferences. Aron sees this as particularly true for HSPs because they react more strongly. Therefore they behave neurotically in an adverse environment but blossom in a supportive one.

There are echoes in the brief description of HSPs above of the preferences for I, S, N and F, which raises the central and long-standing issue in personality theory: what are the most useful ways to describe personality? The preferences and the Big Five factors are two successful solutions and a better one may well emerge in time. Language is a problem; for example, Aron describes HSPs as more conscientious than other people but I interpret her as meaning ethical rather than orderly and so on, as in the Big Five factor of conscientiousness. Similarly, she uses 'sensitive' to mean both caring and touchy.

For now, I think the concepts of High Sensitivity and anxiety may at some point merge to create a clearer quality, and in this book I provisionally call that quality preference for W (Worrying). Perhaps the main contribution of the concept of High Sensitivity to W will be that HSPs feel *positive* emotions more than other people as well as being more vulnerable to negative factors, from troubled childhoods and current conflict to anxiety and depression.

Genetic predisposition provides a way of thinking about these issues of personality characteristics and semantics. Hundreds of genes affect personality and each person has different combinations to give different 'flavours' of each quality. Complicating matters further, the genes interact with each other and with the environment. Thus a particular client or counsellor can usefully be described, given current knowledge, as preferring W (for example) but will do so in their own way because of all the combinations of genetic and environmental factors.

Consider whether pressures early in life or now are relevant

For example, does your client believe that a good woman or man (or many other social categories) tends to have a certain preference? Does your client believe she or he *should* have a particular preference?

Consider using brief exercises

Brief exercises are discussed in Lawrence and Martin (2001) and Bayne (2005). For example, for S versus N, show your client a picture – many of Dali's images work well, as do most pictures with some complexity and ambiguity – and ask what they see. First reactions of people with a preference for S tend to be more detailed and literal; those with a preference for N more of an overview and more inferential and speculative.

Consider using Keirsey's ideas about the four temperaments

The four temperaments are used as a starting point by some experienced MBTI practitioners. Temperament theory illustrates an interactive level of preference theory. It goes beyond a simple additive model, assuming that the preferences for J and P have a major effect on people who prefer S and a minor effect on people who prefer N, and that the preferences for T and F have a major effect on people who prefer N and a minor effect on people who prefer S. These assumptions give four temperaments: SP, SJ, NT and NF. Each temperament includes four of the 16 types. However, although the temperaments are widely used by MBTI practitioners, there has been much less research on them than on the preferences (Keirsey, 1998; Myers et al., 1998).

The four temperaments are represented in the stick figures shown in Figure 2.1. A way of using them is to rank them from most like you to least

40 THE COUNSELLOR'S GUIDE TO PERSONALITY

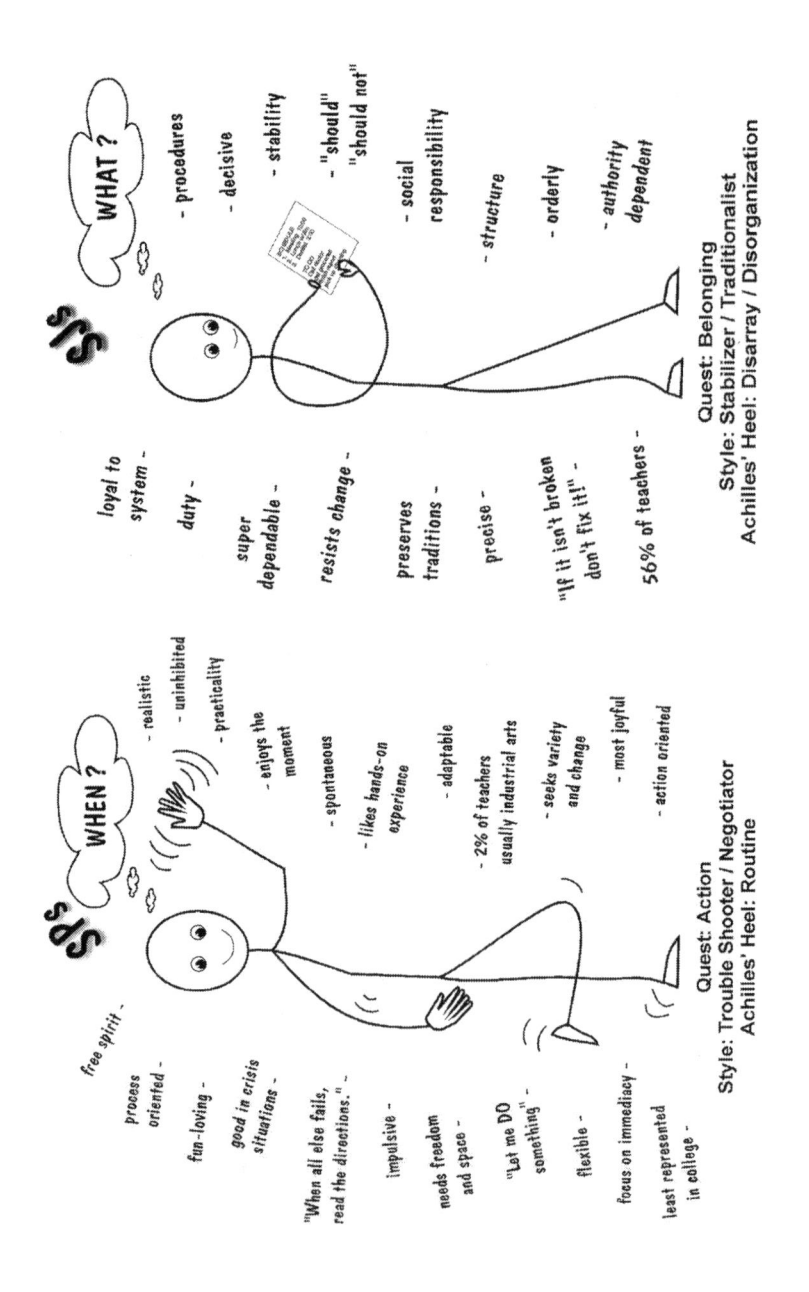

SJs

WHAT?

- procedures
- decisive
- stability
- "should" / "should not"
- social responsibility
- structure
- orderly
- authority dependent

- loyal to system
- duty
- super dependable
- resists change
- preserves traditions
- precise
- "If it isn't broken don't fix it!"
- 56% of teachers

Quest: Belonging
Style: Stabilizer / Traditionalist
Achilles' Heel: Disarray / Disorganization

SPs

WHEN?

- realistic
- uninhibited
- practicality
- enjoys the moment
- spontaneous
- likes hands-on experience
- adaptable
- 2% of teachers usually industrial arts
- seeks variety and change
- most joyful
- action oriented

- free spirit
- process oriented
- fun-loving
- good in crisis situations
- "When all else fails, read the directions."
- impulsive
- needs freedom and space
- "Let me DO something"
- flexible
- focus on immediacy
- least represented in college

Quest: Action
Style: Trouble Shooter / Negotiator
Achilles' Heel: Routine

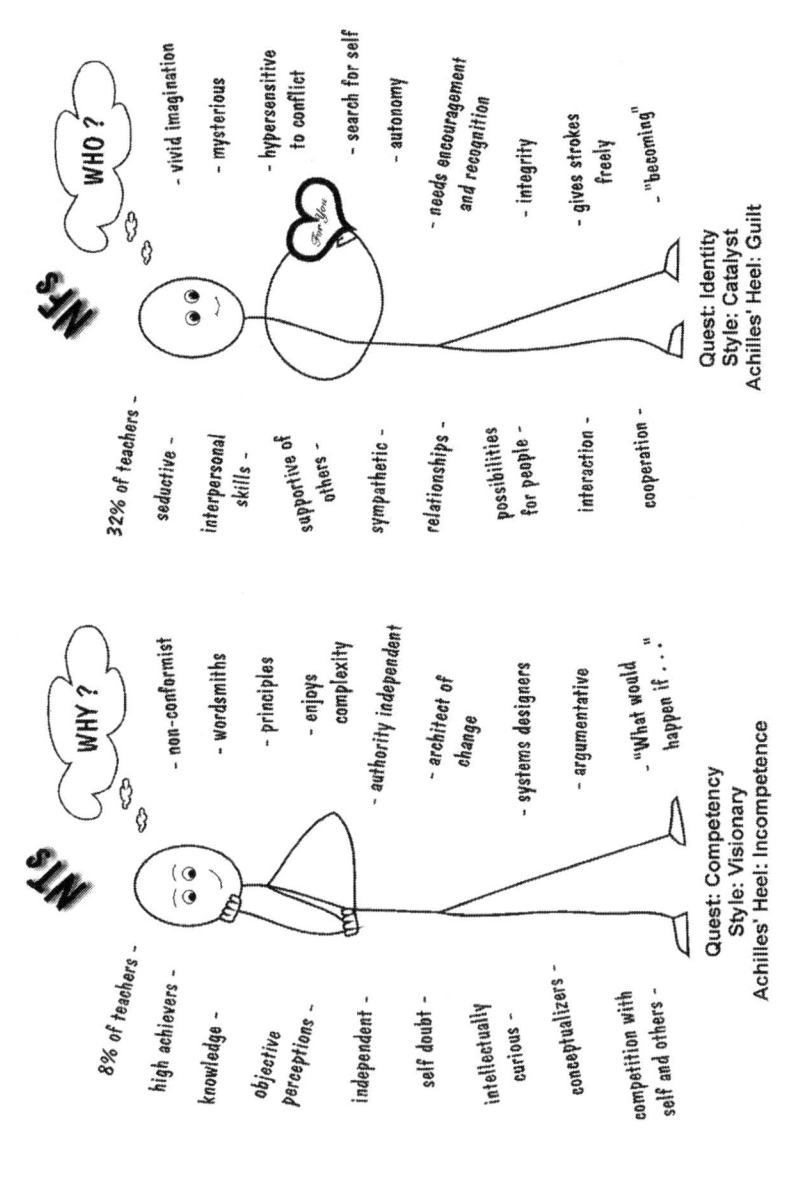

INCREASING SELF-AWARENESS 1: DISCOVERING THE PREFERENCES **41**

NTs

WHY?

- 8% of teachers
- high achievers
- knowledge
- objective perceptions
- independent
- self doubt
- intellectually curious
- conceptualizers
- competition with self and others
- non-conformist
- wordsmiths
- principles
- enjoys complexity
- authority independent
- architect of change
- systems designers
- argumentative
- "What would happen if..."

Quest: Competency
Style: Visionary
Achilles' Heel: Incompetence

NFs

WHO?

- 32% of teachers
- seductive
- interpersonal skills
- supportive of others
- sympathetic
- relationships
- possibilities for people
- interaction
- cooperation
- vivid imagination
- mysterious
- hypersensitive to conflict
- search for self
- autonomy
- needs encouragement and recognition
- integrity
- gives strokes freely
- "becoming"

Quest: Identity
Style: Catalyst
Achilles' Heel: Guilt

Figure 2.1 Source: Temperament stick figures. © 2010 OKA (Otto Kroeger Associates)

like you. Some people find it easier to start with 'least like' and some assign a percentage to each of the temperaments. There haven't been any formal studies of the validity of the stick figures or of these ways of using them.

Consider using a questionnaire

The strongest argument *against* using questionnaire measures of the preferences is that sometimes the answers are taken too seriously, as telling us definitively who we are. In addition, the questionnaire for which there is most evidence, the Myers-Briggs Type Indicator (MBTI), requires specialist training, including an exam, before it can legally be used. The publishers of the MBTI are very protective of it, and in particular keen to prevent misuse.

There are many questionnaire measures of personality – Big Five, psychological type and other theories – on the Internet, including the MBTI itself at www.aptinternational.org. This website includes a clarifying/verifying procedure. Many of the other type questionnaires on the Internet are free but of unknown quality – no details are available of their development or of research on their validity.

The best free questionnaire measure of the preferences is the Keirsey Temperament Sorter II, at www.keirsey.com. Again, the results are useful clues, but probably not as accurate as the MBTI itself. On average, as mentioned earlier, the MBTI is about 75% accurate in the sense that this proportion of people agree with their scores on all four preferences after formal verification (Myers et al., 1998: 116). Ninety per cent agree with three of their preferences. I think 75% and 90% are remarkably high figures given the difficulties of measuring personality.

There are a number of very brief questionnaires for measuring the Big Five. Contrary to the dominant view in psychometrics for many years that long questionnaires were essential for consistent measurement, recent research has found that questionnaires with only two or three items per characteristic work quite well. An example is in Nettle (2007: 271), which has 12 items to measure the Big Five. He gives permission to copy and use it with acknowledgement (2007: 273) but adds that a longer questionnaire is available, also free, at http://ipip.ori.org/ipip.

Read brief descriptions of the whole types

The descriptions in Table 2.6 are indeed brief, and they include the dubious term 'psychic', but nevertheless are a useful first look at whole types. Look for the best fit rather than a perfect fit – people are complicated!

The descriptions don't include the preferences for W (and possibly C) because the descriptions of what would be 32 (or 64 types with C) haven't been developed yet. The current descriptions in Tables 2.6 and 3.2 largely and deliberately describe people at their best, with good development of their preferences. They appear to assume that anxiety is a problem rather than a personality characteristic and thus in effect to be describing people who prefer C. If so, another 16 descriptions of each MBTI type plus W will be needed. This might be too daunting and just too large to use easily. The best solution for now (for this strategy) seems to be to focus on the descriptions of the 16 types while keeping in mind the preferences for C and W as further central qualities which may interact with the other preferences.

Read longer descriptions

Gordon Lawrence's descriptions of the 16 types are in Chapter 3 (Table 3.2) because he chose to emphasise motives and values more than behaviour.

The best validated descriptions of the 16 types are in the sixth edition of *Introduction to Type* (Myers, with Myers and Kirby, 1998). They were developed in several stages (Myers et al., 1998: 119):

- Descriptions from Isabel Myers' earlier descriptions and those of five other authorities were made into a questionnaire.
- Five or six people of each psychological type who (a) had verified their types but (b) were not experienced with type, answered the questionnaire.
- Thirty experts on type commented on the questionnaire items.
- Highly rated descriptions from several studies were added.

The descriptions were then organised into three sections: each type at its best; how others may see them; potential areas for growth.

There are many other, longer, descriptions of the 16 types and each has proved vital for someone in deciding on one or more of their preferences, for example, Berens and Nardi (1999), Keirsey (1998), Kroeger and Thuesen (1988), Hirsh and Kummerow (1990), and Myers' earlier descriptions (in the first four editions of *Introduction to Type*, e.g., 1976), which are warmer, less 'glossy' and less packaged. For example, in later editions, her subheading of 'Is this really me?' is replaced by 'Verifying your type'.

Table 2.6 *Source:* Very brief descriptions of the 16 types © OKA (Otto Kroeger Associates)

ISTJ	ISFJ	INFJ	INTJ
'DOING WHAT SHOULD BE DONE'	'A HIGH SENSE OF DUTY'	'AN INSPIRATION TO OTHERS'	'EVERYTHING HAS ROOM FOR IMPROVEMENT'
Organizer – Compulsive	Amiable – Works behind the scenes	Reflective/Introspective	Theory based – Sceptical – 'My Way'
Private – Trustworthy	Ready to sacrifice – Accountable	Quietly caring – Creative	High need for competency
Rules 'n reasons – Practical	Prefers 'doing'	Linguistically gifted – Psychic	Sees world as a chessboard
MOST RESPONSIBLE	MOST LOYAL	MOST CONTEMPLATIVE	MOST INDEPENDENT
ISTP	**ISFP**	**INFP**	**INTP**
'READY TO TRY ANYTHING ONCE'	'SEES MUCH BUT SHARES LITTLE'	'PERFORMING NOBLE SERVICE TO AID SOCIETY'	'A LOVE OF PROBLEM SOLVING'
Very observant – Cool and aloof	Warm and sensitive – Unassuming	Strict personal values	Challenges others to think
Hands-on practicality – Unpretentious	Short-range planner – Good team member	Seeks inner order/peace	Absent-minded professor
Ready for what happens	In touch with self and nature	Creative – Non-directive – Reserved	Competency needs – Socially cautious
MOST PRAGMATIC	MOST ARTISTIC	MOST IDEALISTIC	MOST CONCEPTUAL

ESTP	ESFP	ENFP	ENTP
'THE ULITMATE REALIST'	'YOU ONLY GO AROUND ONCE IN LIFE'	'GIVING LIFE AN EXTRA SQUEEZE'	'ONE EXCITING CHALLENGE AFTER ANOTHER'
Unconventional approach – Fun	Sociable – Spontaneous	People orientated – Creative	Argues both sides of a point to learn
Gregarious – Lives for here and now	Loves surprises – Cuts red tape	Seeks harmony – Life of party	Brinkmanship – Tests the limits
Good at problem solving	Juggles multiple projects/events Quip master	More starts than finishes	Enthusiastic – New ideas
MOST SPONTANEOUS	MOST GENEROUS	MOST OPTIMISTIC	MOST INVENTIVE
ESTJ	ESFJ	ENFJ	ENTJ
'LIFE'S ADMINISTRATORS'	'HOSTS AND HOSTESSES OF THE WORLD'	'SMOOTH TALKING PERSUADER'	'LIFE'S NATURAL LEADERS'
Order and structure – Sociable	Gracious – Good interpersonal skills	Charismatic – Compassionate	Visionary – Gregarious – Argumentative
Opinionated – Results driven Producer – Traditional	Thoughtful – Appropriate Eager to please	Possibilities for people Ignores the unpleasant – Idealistic	Systems planners – Takes charge Low tolerance for incompetency
MOST HARD CHARGING	MOST HARMONIZING	MOST PERSUASIVE	MOST COMMANDING

TWO EXTRA STRATEGIES FOR DISCOVERING THE PREFERENCES OUTSIDE A COUNSELLING SESSION

Experiment with behaving as if you have each preference

Try behaving like someone with one preference for a few hours or more, then like someone with the opposite preference. Observe your degrees of energy and comfort carefully. This strategy can be very effective, but sometimes, especially when very stressed, a 'break' from using your actual preference can be welcome and therefore misleading.

Ask people who know you well

Show a close friend or relative the 2–4 most likely descriptions. Those in Chapter 3 (Table 3.2) may be the optimum length, and choosing between all 16 seems likely to be too much information to hold in mind in order to make comparisons well, though this hasn't been formally tested.

REPLIES TO QUESTIONS ABOUT PREFERENCE THEORY AND THE PROCESS OF DISCOVERING PREFERENCES

Here are some replies to questions about preference theory which you or your clients may ask.

Question: I vary according to the situation I'm in and I don't like being put in a box.

Reply: It's true that people behave differently in different situations. We are flexible, not robots. However, there are consistencies in nearly everyone's behaviour and most people behave consistently and also expect other people to be consistent. For example, we choose friends and partners at least in part because of their personalities in this sense. Terms like 'gentle' and 'logical' are meaningful. When we describe someone as gentle, it means 'tends to behave more gently than most people and in most situations', and not 'never gets angry or abrasive'.

Question: It's still trying to put me in a box?

Reply: In a way, but it's a flexible box and the aim is to help you understand parts of yourself better as an individual, not to pin you down. The idea of preferences is to be freeing and confirming rather than restricting. You can *behave* like people in any of the boxes, though according to the theory with more effort when using a non-preference. Preference and trait theory both assume that some stability of self is a central part of having an identity.

Question: But I'm both gentle and analytical.
Reply: Yes, you can do both but most people prefer one, and it makes a difference to you which it is.
Question: Can I change my preferences?
Reply: Preference theory says that you can change your behaviour but that each preference remains the same throughout life. What changes is how much we develop each preference and non-preference. So extraverts don't become introverts, for example, but can develop their introverted 'side'.
Question: How easy is it to tell what someone's preferences are?
Reply: The research shows clearly that people are generally quite accurate. However, mistakes are made and for a variety of reasons: for example, the person you are observing may have developed any of their non-preferences well and when observed be using it. They may in that situation be behaving in a very logical and detached way but actually prefer Feeling, for example.
Question: How different are people with the same preferences?
Reply: They can be extremely different while still by definition having some fundamental characteristics in common. Upbringing, values, strengths, motives, life stories and other factors all affect behaviour.
Question: Does preference theory work in different cultures?
Reply: It has been very widely used, with the MBTI translated into over 30 languages so far, including Chinese. All cultures in which the MBTI has been used have included people with all the combinations of preferences.
Question: Isn't it just like astrology?
Reply: The evidence for the validity of the preferences is much stronger than the evidence for astrology. However, the aims of the two theories are the same and both have a largely positive, constructive tone and a flexible, complicated view of personality. But the problem with astrology is that after several thousand studies there is no good evidence for its accuracy and considerable evidence against, for example studies in which the researcher gave other people's descriptions to participants

who then rated them as accurate and insightful. Rigorous attempts to find links between astrological sign and occupation have also failed (Dean, 1986–7).

Question: Does everybody have five preferences?

Reply: Some people are, at the very least, hard to assess accurately, by themselves or others. While most people respond positively to the idea of being basically one preference or the other in each pair, with development to varying degrees of both their preferences and their non-preferences, a few seem genuinely not to have one or more of the preferences.

Question: How many people are there with the same preferences as me?

Reply: In two countries, the UK and the USA, data have been collected from representative samples of their general populations. They are of MBTI types rather than verified types (i.e., preferences after feedback with an expert) and didn't include C and W, plus it is possible that some groups of people are under-represented, for example those who don't answer questionnaires or those who have severe mental health problems. Specific figures are available in Kendall (1998) for the UK and Myers et al. (1998) for the USA, and a summary in Bayne (2004). As a rough guide, the least frequent male and female adult types are INFJ and INTJ respectively, each 3% or less of the general population, and the most frequent adult types, roughly 10% or more of each, are ESTJ, ISTJ, ISFJ and ESFJ.

Question: What about constructivist views of personality? Is there really a real self?

Reply: There are problems with the term 'real' but the evidence for the validity of the preferences is strong. In addition, genetic influences on personality are supported by data on identical twins, separated early – sometimes very early – growing up in different environments and yet being much more similar in personality than children brought up in the same family. Also, identical twins brought up apart are about as similar as those brought up together. In contrast, children who are brought up together are often very unlike each other. Steven Pinker has written in detail about this in *The Blank Slate* (Pinker 2002).

Chapter 3

Increasing Self-awareness 2: Discovering Motives

This chapter discusses preference theory and:

- motives and related concepts as a separate domain of personality;
- motives in temperament theory and preference theory;
- motives for becoming a counsellor;
- the idea of 'good counsellors';
- your choice of counselling orientation.

It also discusses:

- personal strivings and two other general ways of discovering motives;
- values and strengths.

Motives have been defined in a variety of ways in psychology and there is no consensus about their meaning, number or how best to assess them (McAdams, 2009). There are also many similar or identical concepts such as needs, personal strivings and values. The area needs the equivalent of Big Five theory to bring order to it.

Winter et al. (1998) argued that motives and traits – in this context the equivalent of preferences – are complementary: that 'motives involve wishes, desires, or goals (often implicit or nonconscious), whereas traits channel or direct the ways in which motives are expressed in particular actions throughout their life course' (1998: 238). Motives therefore offer the possibility of a different and additional understanding of clients and oneself from preferences on their own (Singer, 2005; Romero et al., 2009). For example, while observing that a person tends to behave in a caring and gentle way is part of knowing them, realising that their motivation is guilt rather than a fundamental desire to help others adds considerably to that understanding.

In addition, misunderstandings occur through not understanding *why* someone behaved as they did. For example, X might long to talk to Y who she finds attractive but unattainable. Signs of frustration and visits to places where she apparently has nothing particular to do are readily explained if X tells you about this desire, but otherwise are likely to remain mysterious.

Individual differences in 'core' motives is an important concept in preference theory and especially temperament theory. A closely related distinction that is important in counselling is sometimes called intrinsic versus extrinsic motivation. Intrinsic motivation is about what a person really wants to do in themselves – rather than because others want them to do it or because they've learnt that it's the right thing to want, that is, for extrinsic reasons. An application of this distinction to careers is not relying on financial rewards to motivate those people who are motivated by (say) wanting to help others or to solve intricate problems. Another example is a person who takes a particular career path for many years before realising that it's never been 'right' for them.

In this chapter I first review ideas from temperament theory and preference theory about a diverse set of core motives or needs, and their implications (and those of other motives) for three aspects of counselling: choosing to be a counsellor, the unhelpful myth of there being one way to be a good counsellor and choice of counselling orientation. Then I discuss a current mainstream psychology technique called the Strivings Assessment Questionnaire (SAQ) and outline two other open-ended techniques. Finally, I briefly discuss two concepts closely related to motives: values and strengths. These approaches to helping clients understand their motives better are predominantly humanistic, but the SAQ and 'I want ...' techniques are sentence completions and therefore projective tests (but inexpensive to use).

MOTIVES AND THE FOUR TEMPERAMENTS

Temperament theory as developed by Linda Berens (2000) suggests the following core needs for each of the four temperaments. The assumption is that everyone has all of these needs but that in each temperament one set is dominant. Berens expressed this idea dramatically. She wrote that they are so central that blocking them is like 'psychological death' (2000: 24), that people feel 'light of spirit' when their core needs are met and 'drained of energy' when they are not (ibid.).

A version of the needs at the core of each temperament is listed in Table 3.1. Which is most like the real you? Which next most? And so on. Alternatively, Nardi (1999) suggested putting them in reverse order or choosing the one *least* like you first and then the 'one you could not live without' (1999: 8). The outcome may be, for example, NF with NT secondary and SJ hardly at all. Temperament theory assumes that while each of us has all the core needs, the strength of each need varies widely.

A key point in using the idea of these core needs with a client is that the terms used to characterise them are abstract summaries and therefore are most usefully seen in the context of an individual's life and using descriptions of the temperaments, for example, the stick figures in Chapter 2 and the profiles in Keirsey (1998).

Another alternative to using Table 3.1 as a starting point is to work from the specific to the more general by asking your client to think, perhaps between sessions, of one or more of the most fulfilling or satisfying projects they've ever worked on and to describe those they found particularly rewarding. Then, and only then, consider with your client which if any of the needs associated with the temperaments fits.

A potential problem in Berens's approach is that she sees the core needs as hard to identify because of life's pressures and experiences. Nardi, too, cautioned that one's true self is 'often masked by one's *developed self*' (1999: 8, emphasis in original). The word 'often' is treacherous here because it is potentially a way of protecting the theory if research or experience do not support it. It also detracts from the appealing simplicity of temperament theory. Unfortunately, temperament theory's ideas about motives have not yet been tested empirically, as far as I know. They are, though, consistent with preference theory, which is quite strongly supported by research.

Anecdotally, Kroeger and Thuesen (1988) and others have found temperament theory very helpful in understanding personality. The

Table 3.1 Examples of core motives in the four temperaments

SP	Solving practical problems quickly, expediently and with flair; being free
SJ	Being responsible and useful to a group or community and planning in detail
NT	Designing new theories and models and analysing intricate problems with precision; being competent
NF	Developing an authentic identity, helping other people to do the same; harmony and finding something worth believing in

following observation is a good illustration. But is it true or is it an example of biased observations and memories? They are writing about the way their guests behave around their swimming pool:

- Our SP guests always grab all the pool toys, head right for the water, and invent a new game.
- The NFs spread on the lounge chairs and talk earnestly about life and people.
- The NTs dangle their feet in the water, rib each other, and critique the issues and people in their professions.
- And the SJs always, always find some work to do, like hanging up towels, husking corn, scrubbing the grill or pulling weeds from the garden. (1988: 52)

MOTIVES AND THE PREFERENCES

The descriptions of the preferences in Chapters 1 and 2 include or clearly imply motives as well as likely behaviours and attitudes, for example F and need for harmony, T and need for competence, J and need for closure. Gordon Lawrence's descriptions of the 16 types (Table 3.2) emphasise motives and values deliberately and more than any other set of descriptions so far (Lawrence, 2010).

Lawrence (2009, 2010) discussed changing the language of type descriptions, focusing much more on 16 'kinds of mind' or 'mental frameworks' than on behaviour. The main descriptions written by Isabel Myers and Katherine Briggs emphasise behaviour characteristics of healthy, mature people of each type, but also intersperse statements about the mental frameworks. For example, INFPs are described as 'sensitive, concerned and caring' (behaviour) as well as 'finding structures and rules confining and preferring to work autonomously' (mental frameworks). A problem is that the term 'sensitive', for example, applies to anyone who has *developed* their F, although it is probably most characteristic of INFPs and ISFPs. Lawrence's suggested rewording of the descriptions is to say that INFPs *value* sensitivity and caring.

At the same time, please bear in mind that the mental frameworks influence behaviour, that preference theory assumes that most people develop their preferences more than their non-preferences and that the evidence on validity supports this assumption.

Lawrence designed the descriptions in Table 3.2 partly to be compact enough to be read quickly but mainly to include 'essential values and priorities of each type' (2010: 137) and to 'better highlight the mental frameworks of each type and minimise the risk that readers will see the types as bundles of traits' (p. 138). Moreover, he sees Jung's theory as giving us 'a fresh, comprehensive and powerful theory of motivation' (p. 139). I agree with this emphasis and judgement but, as discussed in Chapter 1, I am much less convinced than Gordon Lawrence by the evidence for type dynamics, one element of which he illustrates with a

Table 3.2 Gordon Lawrence's descriptions of the 16 MBTI 'types', emphasising motives and values

ENTJ	ISFP
Intuitive, innovative ORGANISERS; analytical, systematic, confident; push to get action on new ideas and challenges. Having extraverted THINKING as their strongest mental process, ENTJ's are at their best when they can take charge and set things in logical order. They value: • Analysing abstract problems, complex situations • Foresight; pursuing a vision • Changing, organising things to fit their vision • Putting theory into practice, ideas into action • Working to a plan and schedule • Initiating, then delegating • Efficiency; removing obstacles and confusion • Probing new possibilities • Holding self and others to high standards • Having things settled and closed • Tough-mindedness, directness, task focus • Objective principles; fairness, justice • Assertive, direct action • Intellectual resourcefulness • Driving towards broad goals along a logical path • Designing structures and strategies • Seeking out logical flaws	Observant, loyal HELPERS; reflective, realistic, empathic, patient with details. Shunning disagreements, they are gentle, reserved and modest. Having introverted FEELING as their strongest mental process, they are at their best when responding to the needs of others. They value: • Personal loyalty; a close, loyal friend • Finding delight in the moment • Seeing what needs doing to improve the moment • Freedom from organisational constraints • Working individually • Peace-making behind the scenes • Attentiveness to feelings • Harmonious, cooperative work settings • Spontaneous, hands-on exploration • Gentle, respectful interactions • Deeply held personal beliefs • Reserved, reflective behaviour • Practical, useful skills and know-how • Having their work life be fully consistent with deeply held values • Showing and receiving appreciation

Table 3.2 *continued*

ESTJ

Fact-minded practical ORGANISERS; assertive, analytical, systematic; push to get things done and working smoothly and efficiently. Having extraverted THINKING as their strongest mental process, they are at their best when they can take charge and set things in logical order.

They value:

- Results; doing, acting
- Planned, organised work and play
- Common sense practicality
- Consistency; standard procedures
- Concrete, present-day usefulness
- Deciding quickly and logically
- Having things settled and closed
- Rules, objective standards, fairness by the rules
- Task-focused behaviour
- Directness, tough-mindedness
- Orderliness; no loose ends
- Systematic structure; efficiency
- Categorising aspects of their life
- Scheduling and monitoring
- Protecting what works

INFP

Imaginative, independent HELPERS; reflective, inquisitive, empathic, loyal to ideals: more tuned to possibilities than practicalities. Having introverted FEELING as their strongest mental process, they are at their best when their inner ideals find expression in their helping of people.

They value:

- Harmony in the inner life of ideas
- Harmonious work settings; working individually
- Seeing the big picture possibilities
- Creativity; curiosity, exploring
- Helping people find their potential
- Giving ample time to reflect on decisions
- Adaptability and openness
- Compassion and caring; attention to feelings
- Work that lets them express their idealism
- Gentle, respectful interactions
- An inner compass; being unique
- Showing appreciation and being appreciated
- Ideas, language and writing
- A close, loyal friend
- Perfecting what is important

ESFJ

Practical HARMONISERS, workers-with-people; sociable, orderly, opinionated; conscientious, realistic and well tuned to the here and now. Having extraverted FEELING as their strongest mental process, they are at their best when responsible for winning peoples' cooperation with personal caring and practical help.

They value:

- An active, sociable life, with many relationships
- A concrete, present-day view of life

INTP

Inquisitive ANALYSERS; reflective, independent, curious; more interested in organising ideas than situations or people. Having introverted THINKING as their strongest mental process, they are at their best when following their intellectual curiosity, analysing complexities to find the underlying logical principles.

They value:

- A reserved outer life; inner life of logical inquiry
- Pursuing interests in depth, with concentration

ESFJ (cont.)

- Making daily routines into gracious living
- Staying closely tuned to people they care about so as to avoid interpersonal troubles
- Talking out problems cooperatively, caringly
- Approaching problems through rules, authority, standard procedures
- Caring, compassion and tactfulness
- Helping organisations serve their members well
- Responsiveness to others, and to traditions
- Being prepared, reliable in tangible, daily work
- Loyalty and faithfulness
- Practical skilfulness grounded in experience
- Structured learning in a humane setting
- Appreciation

INTP (cont.)

- Work and play that is intriguing, not routine
- Being free of emotional issues when working
- Working on problems that respond to detached intuitive analysis and theorising
- Approaching problems by reframing the obvious
- Complex intellectual mysteries
- Being absorbed in abstract, mental work
- Freedom from organisational constraints
- Independence and non-conformance
- Intellectual quickness, ingenuity, invention
- Competence in the world of ideas
- Spontaneous learning by following curiosity and inspirations

ENFJ

Imaginative HARMONISERS, workers with people; expressive, orderly, opinionated, conscientious; curious about new ideas and possibilities. Having extraverted FEELING as their strongest mental process, they are at their best when responsible for winning peoples' cooperation with caring insight into their needs.

They value:

- Having a wide circle of relationships
- Having a positive, enthusiastic view of life
- Seeing subtleties in people and interactions
- Understanding others' needs and concerns
- An active, energising social life
- Seeing possibilities in people
- Thorough follow-through on important projects
- Working on several projects at once
- Caring and imaginative problem solving
- Maintaining relationships to make things work

ISTP

Practical ANALYSERS; value exactness; more interested in organising data than situations or people; reflective, cool and curious observers of life. Having introverted THINKING as their strongest mental process, they are at their best when analysing experience to find the logical order and underlying properties of things.

They value:

- A reserved outer life
- Having a concrete, present-day view of life
- Clear, exact facts; a large storehouse of them
- Looking for efficient, least-effort solutions based on experience
- Knowing how mechanical things work
- Pursuing interests in depth, such as hobbies
- Collecting things of interest
- Working on problems that respond to detached, sequential analysis and adaptability

Table 3.2 *continued*

ENFJ (*cont.*)	ISTP (*cont.*)
• Shaping organisations to better serve members • Sociability and responsiveness • Structured learning in a humane setting • Caring, compassion and tactfulness • Appreciation as the natural means of encouraging improvements	• Freedom from organisational constraints • Independence and self-management • Spontaneous hands-on learning experience • Having useful technical expertise • Critical analysis as a means to improving things

ESTP	INFJ
REALISTIC ADAPTERS in the world of material things; good-natured, easygoing; oriented to practical, first-hand experience; highly observant of details of things. Having extraverted SENSING as their strongest mental process, they are at their best when free to act on impulses, responding to concrete problems that need solving. They value: • A life of outward, playful action, in the moment • Being a troubleshooter • Finding ways to use the existing system • Clear, concrete, exact facts • Knowing the way mechanical things work • Being direct, to the point • Learning through spontaneous, hands-on action • Practical action, more than words • Plunging into new adventures • Responding to practical needs as they arise • Seeing the expedient thing and acting on it • Pursuing immediately useful skills • Finding fun in their work and sparking others to have fun • Looking for efficient, least-effort solutions • Being caught up in enthusiasms	People-oriented INNOVATORS of ideas; serious, quietly forceful and persevering; concerned with work that will help the world and inspire others. Having introverted INTUITION as their strongest mental process, they are at their best when caught up in inspiration, envisioning and creating ways to empower self and others to lead more meaningful lives. They value: • A reserved outer life; spontaneous inner life • Planning ways to help people improve • Seeing complexities, hidden meanings • Understanding others' needs and concerns • Imaginative ways of saying things • Planful, independent, academic learning • Reading, writing, imagining; academic theories • Being restrained in outward actions; planful • Aligning their work with their ideals • Pursuing and clarifying their ideals • Taking the long view • Bringing out the best in others through appreciation • Finding harmonious solutions to problems • Being inspired and inspiring others

ESFP	INTJ
REALISTIC ADAPTERS in human relationships; friendly and easy with	Logical, critical, decisive INNOVATORS of ideas; serious, intent, very independent,

ESFP (cont.)

people, highly observant of their feelings and needs; oriented to practical, first-hand experience. Extraverted SENSING being their strongest mental process, they are at their best when free to act on impulses, responding to the needs of the here and now.

They value:

- An energetic, sociable life, full of friends and fun
- Performing, entertaining, sharing
- Immediately useful skills; practical know-how
- Learning through spontaneous, hands-on action
- Trust and generosity; openness
- Patterning themselves after those they admire
- Concrete, practical knowledge; resourcefulness
- Caring, kindness, support, appreciation
- Freedom from irrelevant rules
- Handling immediate, practical problems, crises
- Seeing tangible realities; least-effort solutions
- Showing and receiving appreciation
- Making the most of the moment; adaptability
- Being caught up in enthusiasms
- Easing and brightening work and play

INTJ (cont.)

concerned with organisation; determined, often stubborn. With introverted INTUITION as their strongest mental process, they are at their best when inspiration turns insights into ideas and plans for improving human knowledge and systems.

They value:

- A restrained, organised outer life; a spontaneous, intuitive inner life
- Conceptual skills, theorising
- Planful, independent, academic learning
- Scepticism; critical analysis; objective principles
- Originality, independence of mind
- Intellectual quickness, ingenuity
- Non-emotional tough-mindedness
- Freedom from interference in projects
- Working to a plan and schedule
- Seeing complexities, hidden meanings
- Improving things by finding flaws
- Probing new possibilities; taking the long view
- Pursuing a vision; foresight; conceptualising
- Getting insights to reframe problems

ENTP

Inventive, analytical PLANNERS OF CHANGE; enthusiastic and independent; pursue inspiration with impulsive energy; seek to understand and inspire. Extraverted INTUITION being their strongest mental process, they are at their best when caught up in the enthusiasm of a new project and promoting its benefits.

They value:

- Conceiving of new things and initiating change

ISFJ

Sympathetic MANAGERS OF FACTS AND DETAILS, concerned with people's welfare; stable, conservative, dependable, painstaking, systematic. Having introverted SENSING as their strongest mental process, they are at their best when using their sensible intelligence and practical skills to help others in tangible ways.

They value:

- Preserving; enjoying the things of proven value

Table 3.2 *continued*

ENTP *(cont.)*	ISFJ *(cont.)*
• The surge of inspirations; the pull of emerging possibilities • Analysing complexities • Following their insights, wherever they lead • Finding meanings behind the facts • Autonomy, elbow room; openness • Ingenuity, originality, a fresh perspective • Mental models and concepts that explain life • Fair treatment • Flexibility, adaptability • Learning through action, variety, and discovery • Exploring theories and meanings behind events • Improvising, looking for novel ways • Work made light by inspiration	• Steady, sequential work yielding reliable results • A controlled, orderly outer life • Patient, persistent attention to basic needs • Following a sensible path, based on experience • A rich memory for concrete facts • Loyalty, strong relationships • Consistency, familiarity, the tried and true • First-hand experience of what is important • Compassion, kindness, caring • Working to a plan and schedule • Learning through planned, sequential teaching • Set routines, common sense options • Rules, authority, set procedures • Hard work, perseverance
ENFP	**ISTJ**
Warmly enthusiastic PLANNERS OF CHANGE; imaginative, individualistic; pursue inspiration with impulsive energy; seek to understand and inspire others. With extraverted INTUITION as the strongest mental process, they are at their best when caught in the enthusiasm of a project, sparking others to see its benefits. They value: • The surge of inspirations; the pull of emerging possibilities • A life of variety, people, warm relationships • Following their insights wherever they lead • Finding meanings behind the facts • Creativity, originality, a fresh perspective • An optimistic, positive, enthusiastic view of life • Flexibility and openness • Exploring, devising and trying out new things	Analytical MANAGER OF FACTS AND DETAILS; dependable, conservative, systematic, painstaking, decisive, stable. Having introverted SENSING as their strongest mental process, they are at their best when charged with organising and maintaining data and material important to others and to themselves. They value: • Steady, systematic work that yields reliable results • A controlled outer life grounded in the present • Following a sensible path, based on experience • Concrete, exact, immediately useful facts, skills • Consistency, familiarity, the tried and true • A concrete, present-day view of life • Working to a plan and schedule

ENFP (cont.)	ISTJ (cont.)
• Open-ended opportunities and options • Freedom from the requirement of being practical • Learning through action, variety, and discovery • A belief that any obstacles can be overcome • A focus on people's potentials • Brainstorming to solve problems • Work made light and playful by inspiration	• Preserving and enjoying things of proven value • Proven systems, common-sense options • Freedom from emotionality in deciding things • Learning through planned, sequential teaching • Scepticism; wanting to read the fine print first • A focus on hard work, perseverance • Quiet, logical, detached problem solving • Serious and focused work and play

Source: © CAPT, not to be reproduced without written permission.

Table 3.3 Main motives proposed for sets of three preferences, based on type dynamics and adapted from K. Myers and Kirby (1994)

ESP	'To experience as much as possible; to have unending variety of sensing experience.' (K. Myers & Kirby, 1994: 12)
ISJ	'To form a solid, substantial and accurate understanding of the world around them and their place in it.' (p. 12)
ENP	'To find and explore new possibilities, new and exciting challenges.' (p. 13)
INJ	'To understand their inner intuitive patterns for understanding the world.' (p. 13)
ETJ	'To create logical order in their external world, make their environment rational.' (p. 14)
ITP	'To create logical order internally, to develop rational principles for understanding the world.' (p. 14)
EFJ	'To create harmony and cooperation in their external environment, to facilitate others in getting what they need and want.' (p. 15)
IFP	'To develop their core of values, establish an external life that is congruent with them and help both individuals and humankind fulfil their potential.' (p. 15)

comment in the introduction to each description. However, the value of his descriptions of each set of preferences still stands.

Type dynamics, which is outlined early in Chapter 7, also proposes main motives. However, I think they follow from the sets of three preferences (Table 3.3) without needing the greater complexity of type dynamics as a rationale.

This list can be used in one or more of the same ways as the core needs for the temperaments (Table 3.1).

MOTIVES FOR BECOMING A COUNSELLOR

You may wish to examine Tables 3.1, 3.2 and 3.3 for ideas about why you are were drawn to counselling. You may also wish to go further and ask if those motives which are not fulfilled ethically in counselling are fulfilled in other parts of your life.

The motives suggested for choosing counselling as a career have sometimes been extremely negative, such as being sadistic or socially inhibited. A more balanced view is that there are functional and dysfunctional motives. Thus, Guy (1987) suggested having a natural interest in people as a functional motive, and he saw the dysfunctional motives mainly as extremes of functional ones: for example, experiencing emotional pain may lead to a person being *too* occupied with healing pain in others but will, in moderation, be functional. Similarly, Hawkins and Shohet (2006: 8) recommended 'facing the shadow': that 'It is not the needs themselves, but their denial that we believe can be so costly' (p. 13).

Three kinds of ideas about core needs and motives for being a counsellor can be distinguished (Bayne & Jinks, 2010):

1. *Bleak:* for example, that counsellors have an uncertain sense of identity, seek power over others, are using clients to work on their own problems, are sadistic.
2. *Positive:* for example, enjoying being useful, solving intricate problems, helping others, variety.
3. *Balanced:* that is, the same motive can be negative or positive depending on the degree of compulsiveness and how self–aware the counsellor is (which assumes most people are fundamentally moral). For example, in counselling, wanting to help a client can be expressed negatively and unethically as wanting to rescue them, or, positively, as wanting to help them help themselves.

Awareness of motives is vital because lack of awareness makes it easier to exploit clients (because most people aspire to be good). A key question suggested by Gerald Corey follows from this: 'Whose needs are being met in this relationship, my client's, or my own?' (2005: 37).

Overall, preference theory proposes positive motives which can be fulfilled in ethical ways by counsellors whose preferences and non-preferences are sufficiently developed. If so, it follows that there are several radically different ways of being a good counsellor too.

THE 'GOOD COUNSELLOR'

The idea of an optimal personality for counsellors can be a destructive one, affecting a counsellor's morale and perhaps reducing the numbers of talented applicants for counsellor training. There is a little research on this idea and two main approaches to it. The first approach shows that although some counsellors are much more effective than others, this may be with particular client groups or problems rather than generally, and that no clear personality characteristics of more effective counsellors have been found so far (Okiishi et al., 2003; Ogles et al., 2004).

The second approach is studies of 'master therapists' as nominated by their peers. For example, Jennings and Skovholt (1999) found that these therapists were emotionally receptive and had excellent relationship skills. No surprises there! And they did not find personality characteristics which defined the 'good counsellor' either. Moreover, the qualities noted above may have been why these therapists were nominated in the first place rather than explaining their effectiveness as counsellors.

Preference theory offers a different perspective on the idea of the 'good counsellor'. It is that people of all preferences can counsel well in their own styles and that each preference underlies skills and strengths which can make a distinctive and positive contribution to outcomes. These diverse skills and strengths can be seen most clearly in integrative approaches to counselling and are illustrated in Tables 3.4 and 3.5.

The three-stage model in Table 3.5 is a map or guide enabling counsellors to locate where they are in a session or in relation to a particular problem. Sessions themselves are fluid, moving backwards and forwards between the stages, and the links between preferences and stages are matters of emphasis. Overall, there are good counsellors in a variety of styles and personalities.

MOTIVES AND YOUR CHOICE OF COUNSELLING MODEL OR MODELS

Preference theory and temperament theory predict that counsellors with different preferences will be most fulfilled, energised and effective with different models of counselling. These are tendencies and not prescriptive. On the contrary, counsellors who are in the 'wrong' orientation as

Table 3.4 The ten preferences and associated strengths and weaknesses to work on for counsellors

Preference	Likely strengths	Likely aspects to work on
E	Easy initial contact Helping clients explore a wide range of issues Energy	Silence Helping clients to explore problems in enough depth Premature action
I	Silence Helping clients to explore problems in depth Reflective and calm	Ease of initial contact Helping clients move to action Helping clients explore all their problems
S	Observing details Being realistic Helping clients decide on practical actions	Brainstorming strategies Trusting hunches Keeping the overall picture in mind
N	Seeing the overall picture Brainstorming Trusting hunches	Noticing and remembering details Testing hunches and assumptions Being realistic about possible actions
T	Being objective Challenging (i.e., offering ideas or new perspectives from the counsellor's frame of reference) Use of theory	Being warmer Premature challenging Empathising sufficiently with the client's emotions Over-use of theory
F	Being warm Being empathic	Challenging Becoming too involved emotionally
J	Being organised Being decisive	Being flexible Being patient
P	Being flexible Being open to new aspects	Being organised Preparing for sessions
C	Being optimistic Being calm	Appreciating that some (most?) clients worry more than you and that this can be a good thing Accepting the more intense emotions of some (most?) clients
W	Being sensitive to threats and risks Feeling emotions intensely	Develop ways of staying calm Develop ways of self-care, e.g. between clients

Table 3.5 Stages of counselling and the preferences most relevant to each

Stages of counselling	Most relevant preferences
Stage 1: Explore The counsellor accepts and empathises with their client and is genuine. The client shares his or her emotions, thoughts, behaviour and experiences about one or more problems.	E, I, S, F, P, C
Stage 2 (if necessary): Understand The counsellor suggests, or helps their client to suggest, themes and new perspectives.	N, T
Stage 3 (if necessary): Action The counsellor helps the client decide what action to take, if any, taking costs and benefits for self and others into account and evaluating the outcomes.	E, S, T, F, J, P, C, W

predicted by theory may contribute in an unusual and valuable way to developing it, or they may be unusually versatile or in a period of developing their non-preferences. The last of these possibilities is more likely to be ethically questionable (back to Corey's key question in the section on motives for being a counsellor).

There is some evidence, both research (Topolinski & Hertel, 2007) and anecdotal, supporting the idea that a good fit between personality and model increases 'job satisfaction'. Windy Dryden gave a particularly good example when he wrote:

> With respect to temperament, I tend to favour an active-directive approach to life and realise now that I felt constrained by the active but relatively non-directive approach advocated by person-centred therapy and by the relatively inactive and neutral style advocated by psychodynamic therapy. REBT also resonated closely with my own natural problem-solving tendencies. (1998: 42)

He added that

> I experience a sense of genuineness when I practise REBT that I never experienced when practising PCT and (fleetingly) psychodynamic therapy.... I could never become an effective person-centred or psychodynamic practitioner because I could not personally resonate

with the central tenets of these approaches. This realisation was painful, but ultimately fruitful. (1998: 43)

Empirically, the relationships between the eight MBTI preferences and choice of orientation found by Nick Dodd and myself (Dodd & Bayne, 2006) and others are moderately strong and can be useful guidelines. Table 3.6 shows the preferences of our sample of 123 experienced counsellors – their average age was early to mid-fifties and typically they had 12 to 13 years' experience. Fifty-five per cent of the counsellors were NFs compared with the UK norm of 14%.

Table 3.7 shows the relationships between the preferences and choice of CBT as an orientation. Seventy per cent of those who chose CBT were SJs. According to temperament theory, SJs are practical, realistic and disciplined, which seems a good description of part of the CBT approach. However, counsellors with other preferences chose CBT too and may well have been fulfilling different motives. The INTJs, for example, are probably enjoying the problem-solving element, the rich variety of irrational beliefs and replacing them through debate with rational ones. (However, the recent emphasis in CBT on being mindful of irrational beliefs rather than replacing them may appeal less to INTJs.)

The other strongest positive relationships were that 38% of the psychoanalytic counsellors were INFJs and 54% of the psychosynthesis counsellors were INFPs. There were many quite strong negative relationships too; for example, 0% INFJs among the CBT counsellors and 8% SJs among the psychosynthesis counsellors. Such findings may help individual counsellors and applicants for training make earlier and better choices about their orientations.

Table 3.6 MBTI preferences (%) of experienced counsellors (N = 123)

ISTJ	ISFJ	INFJ	INTJ
5	12	14	4
ISTP	ISFP	INFP	INTP
0	3	16	0
ESTP	ESFP	ENFP	ENTP
0	2	15	1
ESTJ	ESFJ	ENFJ	ENTJ
3	13	10	1

Table 3.7 Preferences (%) of experienced CBT counsellors (N = 23)

ISTJ	ISFJ	INFJ	INTJ
13	22	0	9
ISTP	ISFP	INFP	INTP
0	4	9	0
ESTP	ESFP	ENFP	ENTP
0	0	4	0
ESTJ	ESFJ	ENFJ	ENTJ
9	26	4	0

The rest of this chapter returns to approaches to discovering motives rather than discussing their effects.

DISCOVERING PERSONAL STRIVINGS

Personal strivings are what we typically try to do or want to try to do in our everyday behaviour (Emmons, 1986; Romero et al., 2009). Like preferences, they assume some consistency. In this approach to discovering motives, there is no concern with how successful or not the strivings are and this is emphasised when introducing the Strivings Assessment Questionnaire (SAQ). A client can complete this questionnaire either verbally or in writing during a counselling session or between sessions.

The SAQ is very straightforward in form. The sentence stem 'I typically try to …' is completed several times (say 10–15). Next, the person's reactions to doing this can be discussed and then they rate each personal striving. The original researcher (Emmons) used 16 scales for these ratings. However, three scales seem enough, at least to begin with. Singer (2005: 52) recommends using a 0–6 scale (where 6 is high), and three criteria similar to these:

- how committed they are to each striving;
- how rewarding they find it;
- how difficult they find it.

Another criterion, with a hint of Berens' 'psychological death', is to ask 'How *essential* is it for you?' The aim is to reveal how a person thinks about their goals and therefore indicate their core motives, clarify them and at some point perhaps challenge them.

More complicated ratings can be used, as indicated above: for example, degree of ambivalence about each striving and how good your client thinks are the chances of achieving it, but I think there's a point of diminishing returns, or even negative returns, though this would vary considerably for different clients and for clients with different preferences. NTs on average would be more likely to seek and enjoy increasing complexity, Ss and Fs least.

An example of responses to an SAQ:

1. Become more extraverted – less timid with the people I know
2. Not be dominated (bullied?) by H
3. Take more pleasure in everyday small things
4. Eat less chocolate
5. Answer my emails more quickly
6. Re-read all of John Updike's books
7. Help my sisters more
8. End with my scary counsellor
9. Phone my parents once a week, at least
10. Take more pleasure in everyday things

The analysis might, for example, show a relationship between how rewarding a striving is to the person and how difficult it is. The key general question is what the whole activity tells the client and counsellor that adds to knowing their preferences. Singer (2005: 58) gives the example of a client who (translating from Big Five factors) prefers F and W. Some of her personal strivings suggest to him that she is trying to manage her tendency to worry, especially her social anxiety – she finds her social world threatening – and that she has a child-like relationship with her family. He wonders, too, if she avoids intimacy with others.

A collaborative approach might be more effective here but this example illustrates the richness of understanding that can begin to develop through the SAQ. Client and counsellor might also choose to consider whether any of the client's strivings are in conflict with each other. If they are, their well-being is probably at greater risk (Emmons & King, 1988).

Personal strivings are obviously a more individual level of personality than the preferences as a starting point for exploration, although the preferences do lead to individual insights too. Conflicting strivings also sometimes explain why two people with the same preferences feel very different.

Conversely, when two people of different types feel a strong connection, they may share a core striving or other motive which they express differently – for example, a need to nurture could be expressed through analysis and logic by an ISTJ and through empathy and compliments by an INFP. As these examples show, analysing the results of measures like the SAQ can become very subtle and time-consuming. There is therefore a risk of over-analysis and neglecting the action stage of counselling.

TWO GENERAL METHODS FOR DISCOVERING MOTIVES

The first method is a variation of the SAQ:

Step 1

Very quickly write 100 statements completing the stem 'I want …'. Repetition is allowed.

Step 2

Analyse the activity and particularly the 100 statements. Did your client answer freely? Are any wants repeated? Are any surprising? Are any enlightening? What do they tell your client about their motives?

The second method is more elaborate:

Step 1

Write a list of all the things you'd like to have but don't have at present – anything at all, including feelings and possessions. No time limit: take as long as you like to write the list.

Step 2

Prioritise each item on the list as most desired, next most desired and so on.

Step 3

Explore how each of the top-rated items, say the top five, would change your life if you achieved it. What difference would it make?

Step 4

Perhaps explore the next five highest rated items.

Step 5

What motives seem most prominent? How much do they feel as if they're from you? This is the key step: uncovering possible core motives.

Step 6

Do you still want the items on the list as much as when you rated them as most desirable etc.?

Step 7

Choose one item, brainstorm possible ways of moving towards achieving it, and devise an action plan.

VALUES AND STRENGTHS

Values are fairly stable beliefs about what matters and doesn't matter. Knowing what your values are can be crucial for making good decisions and counsellors can help clients clarify their values and decide on which are their main values. As with motives, there is the question of which values are a client's own and which imposed or adopted unthinkingly. This distinction is parallel to intrinsic versus extrinsic motives, and, more broadly, to real and false selves.

There are many techniques for clarifying values – for example, laddering (Fransella & Dalton, 2000), in which you ask your client the question, 'What is it about X that is important to you?', then ask the same question of their answer and so on until no more answers are given or your client has had enough. Laddering requires considerable self-awareness – and for many people, patience – but Eleanor Patrick's experience was that she discovered several values 'stumbling around ownerless' and that this felt very positive. She found the process particularly helpful for choosing a model of counselling and for identifying sources of discomfort (Patrick, 2003).

Alex Linley's (2008) definition of strengths was discussed in Chapter 1, in the section on the concept of preference. He used the term 'authentic' (the real versus false distinction again) but emphasised enjoyment and energy as further defining qualities. Authentic preferences, motives, values and strengths all share this quality – they energise and feel 'right'. Another similarity is the number of each which are, or can be, 'core' and the reason it is limited to about five strengths – because time and energy are limited (Buckingham & Clifton, 2001; Linley, 2008). It is not possible to do everything well. The same logic applies to values if they are to be acted on, which would seem to be part of being core.

Linley suggests two problems in identifying strengths: that we're not used to talking about them and that in many cases the words to describe them haven't been created yet. His view is that there are 'likely to be hundreds of different strengths, and the majority have yet to be explicitly identified, defined or named' (2008: 16). An example of a strength that has been named is Lift, which is improving the mood of others through being encouraging and optimistic.

Questionnaires can be helpful starting points, though obviously the results can only include strengths which have been identified and named. Free questionnaires are available at: www.viastrengths.org and www.authentichappiness.sas.upenn.edu/ and updates on Linley and his colleagues' work at the Centre for Applied Positive Psychology are reported on www.cappeu.org. Other methods include:

- noticing what you really look forward to doing;
- noticing what you miss doing;
- reading the descriptions of your psychological type and temperament for clues;
- asking other people who know you well.

In this chapter, I've discussed motives as a second domain of modern personality theory. It includes personal strivings, strengths and values as well as the core motives proposed by temperament and preference theory. It can enrich self-awareness, complementing the preferences and offering ideas about what motivates people to become counsellors and to choose particular counselling orientations. In the next chapter, I turn to the counselling relationship and review in detail ways in which the preferences and the core motives can be used to improve it, for example by communicating the core qualities more quickly and deeply.

Chapter 4

Improving the Counselling Relationship

This chapter discusses preference theory and:

- matching counsellors and clients;
- the four 'languages' associated with preferences for ST, SF, NT and NF;
- applying ideas about matching counsellors and clients through collecting feedback, the skill of 'immediacy' and referral;
- how flexible counsellors can be or want to be in their behaviour with their clients (the 'authentic chameleon' issue);
- counselling clients of each preference;
- acceptance, empathy and genuineness;
- marketing yourself as a counsellor and your counselling room.

Preference theory, including the core motives, suggests several ways of improving the counselling relationship: matching counsellors and clients, matching clients and techniques, as a source of strategies for identifying and resolving problems, including those in the counselling relationship itself, and through refining understanding of the core qualities. More generally, it contributes to including what is *right* about your clients rather than focusing wholly or mainly on their problems.

A possible complication to bear in mind is that your client may have developed one or more of their non-preferences more than their corresponding preferences (called 'type falsification' in Chapter 1). A related and more standard question is how well their life suits their preferences. The answer can in itself clarify or resolve a problem.

MATCHING COUNSELLORS AND CLIENTS

The alluring idea of matching counsellors and clients, thereby improving the quality of their relationship and the effectiveness of counselling, is illustrated by such metaphors as 'being in tune' and 'on the same wave length', and conversely, 'no real contact' and 'speaking a different language'. However, putting it into practice is not straightforward, partly because there are hundreds of characteristics that could be important in making a good match – for example, pace, sense of humour, age, gender and other multicultural factors, values and personality. Moreover, there may be a 'factor X' which influences outcome at least as much as those factors already studied or proposed.

Four 'languages'

In general terms, the essence of matching is that 'different types of clients require different treatments and relationships' (Norcross & Wampold, 2011b: 131). I'll consider different kinds of relationship in this section, in particular the ideas of Susan Brock about four 'languages', each most naturally used by people with one of four combinations of preferences (e.g., Brock, 1994; Allen & Brock, 2000). Susan Brock and Judy Allen have found that using the languages skilfully helps build relationships in both sales and health settings. The four languages are:

- ST language, which is brief and concise, keeps to the point, starts at the beginning, emphasises facts and logic, business-like;
- SF language, which is detailed, practical, warm, caring, friendly, personal;
- NF language, which is personal and abstract, enthusiastic, interested in speculating about interesting possibilities and in ideals;
- NT language, which is impersonal and abstract, critical, reasoned, calm, interested in theory, the long term and your competence.

Brock calls matching the other person's language when your own language is different 'flexing', and her focus is on verbal communication. Communication can also be helped by 'flexing' non-verbally (VanSant, 2003), for example sitting or standing closer to Es, breaking eye contact more with Is, being informal with Ps. Such adjustments may sound minor or odd but VanSant uses the analogy of learning a few phrases of another person's language (in the sense of French, German and so forth), which is usually much appreciated by the native speaker. At the same time, the other person may be irritated by your attempts at using their language, and may see you as false or ingratiating, so how you flex and what behaviour you flex is a very skilful and artistic judgement.

Judy Provost has a more complex approach to matching languages than Brock's – she wants counsellors to 'talk 16 types' (1993: 24). But she is an ENFP! She also makes a subtle point about matching, saying that at the same time as matching their clients, counsellors 'should be themselves' and that 'Although counselors can build rapport by mirroring clients' types, this does not mean that counselors should or can "become" the client's type. Counselors should be themselves and work from their strengths. Talking a client's type is only the first step to reach a client' (1993: 26). Here Provost is implying that counsellors may use different languages with the same client at different stages of counselling, an idea consistent with the three-stage model of counselling (see Table 3.5), and with the 'stages of change' model.

Stages of change

In the stages of change model, five stages (sometimes four, omitting Preparation) are generally distinguished (Norcross et al., 2011):

1. *Precontemplation* – the person is reluctant to be a client and usually doesn't see themselves as having any problems. They are at best doubtful about the value of counselling, at least for themselves. Other people may persuade them to try it.
2. *Contemplation* – the person recognises that they have a problem or problems and have thought seriously about possible solutions.
3. *Preparation* – intending to take action soon.
4. *Action* – making changes and putting a lot of energy and time into doing so.
5. *Maintenance* – working to prevent 'relapse' but also treating it as normal (though not inevitable) and manageable.

Stage of change is assessed for each of a client's problems by asking directly: 'Would you say you are not ready to change in the next 6 months (precontemplation), thinking about changing in the next 6 months (contemplation), thinking about changing in the next month (preparation) or have you already made some progress (action)?' (Norcross et al., 2011: 151).

This model may seem too obvious, merely saying that counselling is more successful with clients who are ready to change. However, it does more. First, it counteracts the tendency for therapists to assume that clients are ready to change, that is, that they are in stage 3. Indeed, Norcross et al. estimate that only 20% of clients are in stage 3, with about 40% in stage 1 and 40% in stage 2.

Second, it enables a focus on helping clients in stage 1 move forward (if they wish), rather than on a probably futile and perhaps irritating later stage of change. Third, it suggests treating problems in stage 2 gently, because action would often be premature.

Similarly, match kind of relationship and stage of change. Here, Norcross et al. suggest, crisply, 'a nurturing parent stance with a precontemplator, a Socratic teacher role with a contemplator, an experienced coach with a patient in action, and then a consultant once in maintenance' (Norcross et al., 2011: 152). In terms of the preferences this means emphasising F for nurturing, N and T for disputing and so on, and E and J for action (see Table 3.5).

The authentic chameleon issue

An issue that's raised by the three-stage model, the stages of change and the skill of flexing is: how versatile can a counsellor be and still be congruent? For example, Windy Dryden has described putting his feet on his desk and drinking from a can with one client, and putting a tie on and sitting up straight for the next. And Arnold Lazarus, in an interview with Dryden, similarly argued that some clients want a 'somewhat formal, almost austere business-like' approach, not a 'gooey and supportive relationship' (in Dryden, 1991: 18). Lazarus counselled in both of these and other styles, often changing his style with the same client (Lazarus, 1993), but he noted that 'in many instances, it is extremely difficult to articulate the precise reasons for adopting a specific stance at a given moment' (Lazarus, 1993: 406). This is still true nearly 20 years later, but preference theory offers a clearer and fuller rationale.

In the same interview, Lazarus criticised Carl Rogers for lacking versatility, for 'constantly offering his carefully cultivated warmth, genuineness and empathy to all his clients' (Dryden, 1991: 18). He seems to me wrong about 'carefully cultivated', because Rogers behaved like a natural F – but should Rogers have been more versatile? Preference theory states that people with some preferences (in theory, E, N and P all play a part, especially in combination) are more naturally versatile. Dryden took the position that counsellors 'cannot be all things to all clients ... your personality and temperament limit how much you can vary' (2011: 41). However, versatility increases with experience for some counsellors and there is another option implied strongly by preference theory: 'judicious referral' (touched on by Lazarus, 1993, and discussed briefly later in this section).

Collecting feedback and the skill of immediacy

Three factors in deciding when to use a different language or to discuss referral are your judgements of your client's stage of change, their stage of counselling and their preferences. All these can in turn be influenced and aided by feedback from your client and your use of the skill of immediacy.

The idea that systematically and frequently collecting and using client feedback helps develop a therapeutic relationship is strongly supported by Duncan et al. (2010) and Lambert and Shimokawa (2011). Duncan et al. go so far as to say that 'Using formal client feedback to inform, guide and evaluate treatment is the strongest recommendation coming from this volume' (2010: 424) while Lambert and Shimokawa concluded that clinicians should 'seriously consider making formal methods of collecting client feedback a routine part of their daily practice' (2011: 72).

Two explanations for the benefits of using client feedback are that it can counter therapists' tendency to be too optimistic about their clients' progress, and that, used well, it communicates both respect and taking a collaborative approach – 'working with' rather than 'doing to'. It may also help to alleviate the stress for counsellors of clients who leave counselling without warning (Bayne et al., 2008).

On the question of how to discuss client feedback, Swift et al. (2011) recommended that therapists inform clients about the options (if the client wishes), discuss them with clients and if necessary work to help clients express and consider what they'd prefer (again, if the client wishes – some clients want their therapists to choose and this too can usefully be discussed). They noted too that clients may change their minds. Their final recommendation was: 'When a psychotherapist believes that a client's preferences for therapy are not in the client's best interest, share their concern with their client so that treatment decisions can still be made collaboratively' (2011: 164).

Norcross and Wampold (2011b) take a similar approach to the question of what they do if they're unable or unwilling to adapt their approach to a client in ways supported by the research on matching. They recommend one or more of (1) address the matter 'forthrightly', (2) discuss treatment options and choosing between them with their client, (3) choose clients who fit their approach, and (4) 'judicious referral'.

The skill of immediacy is central to how feedback and decisions about aspects of your counselling relationship can be discussed with clients. It is direct, mutual talk (Bayne et al., 2008; Egan, 2010). For example, 'I wonder if you'd like me to speak more often' (perhaps an I counsellor speaking to an E client), or 'What's happening to me as we work together is that I have lots of ideas about what you're saying but I keep quiet about them because often they're only the beginning of ideas or probably silly. I wonder if we could sometimes try using the strengths of *both* our preferences – so I'll say my ideas and you critique/rip into them?' (N counsellor with an ST client).

Referral Preference theory can help make referral more acceptable to both clients and counsellors by reducing feelings of failure and rejection. Indeed it can go much further by reframing referral as a positive step. For example, Windy Dryden wrote: 'I tend to get referred clients whom the referrer thinks need a robust and no-nonsense counsellor, rather than clients who need a lot of gentle coaxing' (2011: 41).

NOTES ON COMMUNICATING WITH CLIENTS OF EACH PREFERENCE

Clients who prefer Extraversion (E) or Introversion (I)

Clients who prefer E tend to want more social chatter and a more active counsellor, and to be less comfortable with quiet reflection. They may think about an Introverted counsellor: 'You're so quiet. I don't know whether to trust you or not.' Conversely, clients who prefer I tend to be more comfortable with silence and reflection, and, perhaps surprisingly, less enthusiastic about counselling.

Nocita and Stiles (1986) contrasted two views about Introverts' experience of being a client in individual counselling: either they would tend to find it uncomfortable or, alternatively, the inward focus might be congenial – more than it is for Es at least. They asked 83 adult clients about the impact of their counselling on them during the sessions. Their main finding was that on average the Is rated their sessions as 'relatively uncomfortable, unpleasant, tense, rough and difficult'. Moreover, their mood after the sessions was rated by them as 'relatively unfriendly, uncertain, sad, angry and afraid' (1986: 235). The effects were substantial. The authors recognised that distress is not necessarily a bad thing during or after counselling, but also that it can lead to a premature ending or be unnecessary. They recommended that counsellors be particularly aware that Introverts are more likely to be uncomfortable.

Es are more likely than Is to stay in contact with you while they speak and to explore and reflect aloud. They are trying out ideas as they speak and may sound as if they're making decisions when they're not. It may be helpful on occasion to interrupt Es, in effect to encourage them to develop their I qualities a little by reflecting quietly. In the same way, it is sometimes helpful to encourage Is to reflect aloud. Provost suggests that Is may wish to write questions and impressions between sessions and then to read them to you during a session (1993: 28).

Among the suggestions from Miller (1991) and Provost (1993) are for Es to be matched with group counselling and with person-centred counsellors (because they tend to talk easily), Is with cognitive counselling, Gestalt counselling, bibliotherapy and writing (because they don't), but of course there are exceptions.

Shy Es Just as there are socially skilled introverts, so there are people who are both shy and have a preference for E. Cheek and Buss (1981) suggested that they are in a state of tension, wanting to mix with other people but fearful of doing so.

Clients who prefer Sensing (S) or Intuition (N)

Timothy Miller wrote about the Big Five parallel of the preference for S or N: 'Some clients are intrigued by an invitation to engage in a conversation with the ghost of their dead grandmother in an empty chair; whereas others find it exquisitely uncomfortable to behave in such a peculiar manner' (1991: 416). Thus clients who prefer S tend to be concrete and practical and not see many options while Ns tend to overlook facts, to like novel and imaginative approaches and to be unrealistic.

A characteristic S way of talking is to lead up to the main point step by step. N counsellors can find this exasperating; they typically want the main point first. But the detail is very important to Ss – and can be pivotal for solving a particular problem. Conversely, Ns tend to leap from topic to topic, which S counsellors may find exasperating (or fun at first, then exasperating).

CBT (cognitive behavioural therapy) may be the most effective orientation for Ss (because they're more practical), dream work and existential therapy for Ns (because they're more abstract). On the other hand, mindfulness-based approaches seem likely to be pointless for developed Ss, especially ESPs and SPs, because they are naturally mindful.

Clients who prefer Thinking (T) or Feeling (F)

Miller wrote about the Big Five parallel of the preference for T or F: 'Some clients are eager to accept the putative wisdom and good intentions of the therapist, but others assume the therapist is a fraud or a fool until they see evidence to the contrary' (1991: 416–17). Here, Miller captures some key tendencies of people who prefer F – to trust and to be eager to please, sometimes becoming dependent (and apparently agreeing with everything you say) – and of those who prefer T – to want proof of competence.

Counsellors may decide to challenge the F tendencies (gently) and benefit, as do their clients, from being ready for T clients to challenge them. Another implication of preference theory for counselling Ts is not to press Ts on their emotions, especially early in counselling, but rather to introduce emotions as a relevant factor at an appropriate time. A counter-intuitive suggestion for matching TF and counselling orientation is that REBT (rational emotive behaviour therapy) will be more effective with Fs, because the Ts will already have tried logic and analysis.

Female Ts Kroeger and Thuesen (1988: 131) suggested that some women who prefer T, which goes against the Western stereotype for women, behave in a compensatory way: they are ultra-feminine, with 'girly' clothes and voices and 'a breathy softness of speech' which seems false (Stokes, 1987a, 1987b). There is nothing wrong with this in itself but from a preference theory perspective they are not expressing their preference for T directly and this 'protective coloration' (Myers with Myers, 1980: 66) will be a strain.

Women who prefer T tend to be seen as more aggressive and hard than men who prefer T and who are behaving in the same way. Barger and Kirby (1993) studied INTP women in a number of cultures and found that they felt they didn't fit in, as adolescents or adults. Similar studies of women of the other types which include a preference for T have not been carried out yet but would probably find a similar effect. About 40% of women in the UK and USA prefer T (research reviewed in Bayne, 2004).

Male Fs Kroeger and Thuesen (1988) suggested that some men who prefer F behave in ultra-macho ways, for example sporting tattoos, motor bikes, leather jackets, dark glasses, a swagger (in some cultures and times). The same caution applies to interpreting these clues as it does to those for the ultra-feminine Ts. Like female Ts, male Fs are a large minority.

Clients who prefer Judging (J) or Perceiving (P)

Clients who prefer J tend to need structure, to work hard and to tolerate discomfort. They may be very afraid of losing control. Clients who prefer P tend to need flexibility and to avoid discomfort and discipline. Miller takes a clear position on Ps: he sees them as poor candidates for counselling and gives several vivid examples. One is of a woman who has hated herself for years because she is overweight. Miller encouraged her to keep an eating diary and calculate her calorie intake. He continued to encourage her to persevere with these strategies. His client explained that 'she is afraid that she will be upset if she learns how much she really eats'. His response was that 'We agree that it might be a good thing if she got upset about her eating habits ... she never complies with the plan' (1991: 430).

I wrote to Timothy Miller about preference theory and its implications for counselling generally and in particular for clients like the one who didn't comply with the plan. I found him very thoughtful and articulate, and firm in his position on clients with a strong preference for P (in my terms) or low on conscientiousness (his). He saw them as very unlikely to change and thinks that therapy with them 'must be primarily palliative or supportive'. However, he was thinking about clients with extremely low scores on conscientiousness (he used a Big Five questionnaire) and he added that 'Outcomes may improve if therapists can learn better how to inspire or cajole them' (1991: 431).

I find Miller's experience and views on Ps very provocative and I don't agree with him; my experience is that Ps respond positively to being appreciated for their strengths and to an approach which is a little J but primarily P, as Judy Provost illustrates in the ENFP case study summarised later in this chapter. My argument was that his strategies were suitable for clients who prefer J but that those who prefer P and who have not developed their J need fundamentally different strategies. This theme is illustrated in Chapter 6, in the sections on dieting and exercise.

Clients who prefer Calm (C) or Worrying (W)

The calmness or 'emotional blandness' (Miller, 1991) of clients who prefer C may be misinterpreted as defensiveness.

People who prefer W are likely to benefit more than Cs from creating or finding environments that suit them and avoiding those that don't; from avoiding people they find draining or upsetting; and from other ways of managing their emotions, such as doing routine tasks quietly, letting their minds rest and wander, not watching the news, and being peaceful. Miller (personal communication, 1994) wrote (and here 'high neuroticism' is the Big Five parallel of preference for W) that in his experience, 'the best response to high neuroticism is to embrace it, respect it, refuse to apologise for it, anticipate discomfort under certain circumstances and adjust one's life accordingly. My clients are surprisingly receptive to this view.'

Because Ws easily become over-aroused, counsellors can help by behaving particularly calmly and gently, and by starting sessions informally so that they can check on their client's level of arousal. Here Elaine Aron suggests looking for avoidance of eye contact, for whether your client is sitting stiffly and for repetitive gestures. Clients who prefer W also tend to be more sensitive to criticism and prone to shame (Aron, 2010).

TWO CASE STUDIES

Judy Provost's 1993 book contains brief case studies (2–3 pages) of her work with clients of all combinations of the eight MBTI preferences. She uses the type dynamics level of MBTI theory, but I find her analyses very engaging and instructive examples of preference theory in action too.

An ISFJ client

This ISFJ client saw herself as a slow learner and her life as dull and no fun, and Provost writes that she controlled her own natural, relatively bold approach (as an ENFP), describing their relationship as a 'series of gentle pushes, cautious tries, and sometimes retreats' (1993: 52). She suspected that if she had worked at her usual pace the client would either have left or become defensive. Occasionally she tried a paradoxical intervention like, 'You're not ready to change – let's be more cautious.'

Provost's respect for her client's strengths – for example, warmth and caring and organisation (developed F and J respectively) – is very apparent. She writes that she learnt to be more patient from this client and that 'mutual respect and fascination with each other's processes were important elements in our counselling relationship' (1993: 52).

An ENFP client

The second example is Provost working with another ENFP. Like many young (and some older) ENFPs, this client's F was undeveloped, as shown by her starting numerous projects with great enthusiasm, not finishing them and becoming very, and understandably, discouraged. She also had a 'whirlwind' social life, another EFP characteristic.

When the client was learning to develop her F, one of the things that worked well for her was to find daily quiet time to go 'inside' and write a stream-of-consciousness journal. Another strategy was for her client to ask herself what was important to her at this moment. Learning to say 'no' to friends and invitations also helped. Gradually these and other interventions resulted in the client feeling much more grounded (while still an ENFP) and in changing her area of study from medicine to English.

THE CORE COUNSELLING QUALITIES

Acceptance

Most counsellors believe in being accepting towards their clients and, particularly if they are person-centred, may well treat acceptance as a way of being which is vital for good counselling. Thus, ideally, we don't judge any emotions, fantasies or other inner aspects of real selves (see Table 1.2) as bad or good because this offers our clients the opportunity to understand and accept themselves more deeply and fully.

Acceptance is difficult in practice because we naturally make judgements and assumptions about what is desirable and normal. Preference theory helps to increase acceptance by extending the range of behaviours, motives and reactions regarded as normal. For example, many books on writing strongly advise sticking to a schedule as a key to being productive, when people with a developed preference for P tend to produce their best work at the last minute. Ps tend to be energised by the pressure of an imminent deadline while Js tend to find the pressure stressful rather than stimulating and consequently try to start early. Both Js and Ps can be equally productive with these radically different approaches.

Another example of bias against the preference for P is the main theme of a book on dieting called *Does This Clutter Make My Butt Look Fat?* (Walsh, 2008). Walsh argued that clutter in the home causes weight gain because it signifies a lack of control. The lack of control is also reflected in the untidiness. Therefore, decluttering, planning and developing routines are the solution to losing weight. The logic and truth of this argument is dubious but it illustrates well the non-acceptance of an aspect of a P way of life.

The opposite bias, which is probably less common, was illustrated eloquently in an article by Simon Barnes in *The Times* (14 October 2011,

p. 25). It began: 'Tidiness is a form of death' and went on to argue for the virtues of untidy desks, houses and farms. About his desk, he wrote that 'it is a living desk and it produces work. I could tidy it up, certainly, but then I wouldn't get any work done. The desk would be sterile.' About farmland, he wrote that 'when you see untidy farmland, you should always remember to cheer. For here is life.' The general point here, putting aside differences between desks and farmland, is that his view is unaccepting of an aspect of preferring J and therefore doesn't do justice to a healthy and effective form of people's individuality.

Counsellors too may be irritated by clients with one or more opposite preferences to their own and may judge such clients to be difficult, immature or even as having a personality disorder when they are just different. Preference theory contributes to greater acceptance by questioning assumptions about what people should be like and by being specific about several very different ways of being happy and effective. Table 4.1 summarises some of the common ways of being unaccepting about (biased against) each preference.

Each of these biases can be reframed positively: for example, 'uptight' as organised and dependable; 'weak-willed' as flexible and adaptable; meek as a core need for harmony; criticism as a core need to improve something or someone. Reframing can also counter misinterpretation of behaviour that is the result of a preference as defensive or resistant. However, reframing can be difficult or impossible to actually do!

It is probably helpful in countering such biases to know your own preferences. A complication is that, occasionally, a client has a negative view of one or more of their own preferences. They may go so far as to long to have the opposite preference. Preference theory, as discussed in Chapter 1 in the section on personality change, assumes that changing preferences

Table 4.1 Some negative perceptions of each preference

E	Loud, intrusive, repetitive, shallow, overwhelming
I	Inhibited, boring, insular, too sensitive, slow
S	Plodding, boring, slow to get to the point
N	Flaky, unrealistic, vague, unfocused
T	Cold, distant, insensitive, critical
F	Illogical, meek, too sensitive, soft
J	Controlling, obsessive, inflexible, judgemental
P	Careless, weak-willed, disorganised, frivolous, messy
C	Reckless, bland, foolish
W	Fussy, tense, too cautious

is not possible in normal circumstances (i.e., excluding brain damage, some illnesses etc.). The best approach for a counsellor to take with such 'preference envy' is first to check how their client defines the preference. My experience is that often the client has an inaccurate idea about their preference: for example, they've learned that Es are shallow and loud whereas preference theory says they tend to be expansive and energetic. Alternatively, the client can choose to develop their non-preference more than their preference and accept the resulting 'type falsification' (discussed briefly in Chapter 1).

Empathy

Preference theory illustrates in a very concrete way how difficult it is to be empathic. According to the theory, it is impossible to *really* understand what it is like to have an opposite preference to our own, even though we use all our preferences and non-preferences. But knowing this limitation and knowing how profoundly people differ may make genuine empathy more likely and also happen more quickly and deeply. In part, this is because the widespread belief that 'people are like me' becomes less of an obstacle. The belief is more consciously present and can therefore be more readily countered. Of course, counsellors are experienced in empathising with a wide variety of people already and so are aware of large personality differences; what preference theory adds is (1) being specific about the central, most important differences, (2) the extent of those differences, and (3) positive interpretations of them.

For example, when I was listening to an SJ client talking about pressure of work, temperament theory suggested to me that the core motive of being responsible would be central in her life and not in mine, because I am an NF. If I had not known that my client was a developed SJ (and that I am not) then I might well have taken longer to understand this quality in her, or failed to accept it and empathise with it at all. Much worse, I might have challenged it as an intrinsically unfulfilling way to be and in effect encouraged her to be a P (like me). This, of course, would have been deeply unempathic and she might not have returned for further sessions.

The accepting approach to this client, using preference theory and a model of counselling that includes support and challenge, is first to empathise with her central need to feel responsible and her weariness, then, at the right time and if she doesn't challenge herself, gently challenge her with the idea that it is possible to be *too* responsible and that, while still being a responsible person, she might like to consider developing her P side *a little*.

A deeper failure of empathy would have occurred with this client if I had misunderstood her motive as too great a need to please others. Another failure would have been to suggest being more P and then to miss her negative reaction. That is, temperament theory assumes that she really and naturally feels a deep sense of duty and responsibility and introducing much less routine say (as part of developing her non-preference for P) might demoralise or shock her, in the same way that someone who prefers P might well be unenthusiastic, at the least, about much more routine and planning.

Empathy is defined in a wide variety of ways by theorists and by counsellors, and many attempts have been made to bring greater clarity. Susy Churchill used preference theory in her own attempt (Churchill & Bayne, 1998) and interviewed experienced counsellors about their approach. One of her questions was: 'When you're actually with a client, how do you come to understand what's going on for your client?' You might like to pause at this point and write your answer to this question.

The most obvious hypothesis was that T counsellors would talk about empathy in a cognitive way and Fs in an affective way. We failed to find strong support for this but explained it as the effects of counsellor training. We suspect there is a real relationship between T and cognitive empathy and so on which would be evident in counselling sessions themselves but we appreciate that this suspicion needs to be tested!

We did find differences between (a) preference for S and statements by counsellors about empathy as a *state*, such as references to 'being with them' and 'moment by moment', contrasting with preference for N and *process* statements like 'deeper levels of empathy'; and (b) preference for J and *active* statements like 'trying to tune in', 'putting different bits of information together' and really wanting to know this person', contrasting with P and *passive* statements like 'being receptive' and 'experiencing it with them'.

For us, a particularly interesting aspect of the research was that the preferences had a much greater effect than the counsellors' orientations on their views of empathy. For example, the two ISTJ participants were respectively cognitive and psychodynamic in orientation while the two INFPs were person-centred and integrative, yet in their interviews the ISTJs emphasised a drive to plan the therapy, define the problems and identify goals while the INFPs stressed fully entering their client's world.

For counsellors, the implication is that clients of different preferences are likely to respond most to different kinds of empathy, and at different stages of change and counselling. For counsellor trainers, it is to be aware of bias in how we define, give feedback on and assess empathy.

Genuineness

Genuineness, congruence, self-actualisation, 'finding one's real self', being true to oneself and authenticity are similar or identical ideas, and quite vague and abstract (especially, in Keirsey's view, to SPs, SJs and NTs). However, Abraham Maslow, who wrote extensively about self-actualisation (e.g., Maslow, 1968), defined it partly in terms of individual differences in personality and potential and partly as behaviour. For example, he suggested that one way a person self-actualises is by experiencing their reaction to something fully, vividly and with total concentration and then, if appropriate, expressing it (Smith et al., 2012). Maslow further suggested that most people rarely do this. Instead, when asked our view of something, we try to impress, to entertain, to be tactful or kind or to fit in. He saw the consequence as widespread self-alienation, with the underlying real selves continuing to press for actualisation.

The model of self and self-awareness depicted in Table 1.2 implies at least three meanings of genuineness. The first is represented by Abraham Maslow, the second by Carl Rogers and the third by Isabel Myers and preference theory. Their differences and similarities in this respect are compared in Table 4.2.

Thus, Carl Rogers saw real selves as fluid but he agreed with Maslow about the prevalence of self-alienation (incongruence). Dave Mearns and Brian Thorne put this position strongly: 'Incongruent relating is so thoroughly ingrained within our culture that it has become viewed as the healthy and even sophisticated reality. As human beings we use our considerable skills to cultivate our incongruence such that we are protected from being truly seen by the other' (2007: 120).

In contrast, for Isabel Myers (and preference theory and Big Five theorists and researchers), real selves are both fluid and include stable personality characteristics, and most people are not self-alienated. However, most of us may be less aware of fluid aspects of our selves than of our preferences, while benefiting from being clearer about what they mean and their value.

Table 4.2 Three meanings of genuineness

Fluid or stable core self, or both?	Expressed genuinely by most people or self-alienation more prevalent?
Maslow: Both	Self-alienation
Rogers: Fluid	Self-alienation
Myers: Both	Genuine

Some rapprochement between these three or more meanings of genuineness seems possible but this is the most complicated of the core counselling qualities, with much left to clarify about the most useful definition and the artistic aspects of being or using it well. For counselling practice, genuineness is obviously central to developing trust, to immediacy and to counsellor self-disclosure (Mearns & Thorne, 2007; Bayne et al., 2008; Smith et al., 2012). The contribution of preference theory, and more broadly the model of self in Table 1.2, is to propose specific elements of fluid and stable selves to be genuine about or alienated from.

MARKETING YOURSELF AS A COUNSELLOR

Some counsellors find marketing, especially marketing themselves, unappealing. Indeed, preference theory suggests that most counsellors will feel this way, because most counsellors prefer F. It is also consistent with Fs earning less than Ts (Judge et al., 2012). However, potential clients need to find out about counsellors and marketing helps them to do this. It may help counsellors to think of it not as selling but as 'telling people what I do to be helpful' (Bayne et al., 2008). Moreover, there is an artistic, self-expression element in designing publicity materials, websites and so forth which could also make 'marketing' more appealing.

Professional marketing people use personality theory to 'target' (an interesting marketing term!) the customers they want. A question you may wish to consider in creating or commissioning marketing materials is whether you would rather work with clients of some preferences or temperaments than others. You may also wish to bear in mind the high proportion of clients, as well as counsellors, who prefer N and F (Myers et al., 1998).

Another issue is, given the large proportion of SJs and SPs in the general population (about 75%), do you want to advertise in ways that attract or at least do not deter potential clients with these preferences? You would also help more people because Ss tend to be practical and to live more in the present, so when they do go for counselling it tends to be short term.

The 'languages' of ST and SF as described in Chapter 4 should be helpful in making these decisions and in creating websites, leaflets and other marketing/publicity material, as should informal (or formal) market research. The standard reference on the preferences and selling which uses the four languages of ST, SF, NT and NF is Brock (1994). I recommend that if you choose to target clients of particular preferences or temperaments, consult people who have those preferences. Their reactions to your

Table 4.3 The preferences and writing

Preference	Strengths	To add later
E	Talking about the topic, starting writing, fluent	Organising, rewriting
I	Silent reflection, immersing yourself in the material	Actually write! (don't wait too long)
S	Detail and examples	Themes, delete some of the detail
N	Lots of ideas	Examples, delete some of the ideas
T	Objective style and logical sequence	Personal touches and warmth, tact and flow
F	Best at writing about topics which you care about	Evidence, analysis
J	Start early, firm conclusions	Appropriate caution, questions
P	Lots of material and angles, revising	Selecting, conclusions
C	Confidence, adventure	Appropriate caution, balance
W	Aware of potential problems and risks	Appropriate boldness, balance

drafts and approach to marketing (and your counselling room – see next section) are likely to be surprising and very useful.

When writing materials for clients and potential clients, preference theory suggests using the strengths of your preferences first and adding your non-preferences later. The strategies implied by this principle are summarised in Table 4.3.

YOUR COUNSELLING ROOM

The room or office you use for counselling (although some therapists walk and play tennis etc. with some of their clients) is likely to appeal much more to some of your clients than others, perhaps even deterring some. One client will see a brightly lit room, piles of papers and books and a beard as welcoming; another will see them as unprofessional. How warm – in the interpersonal sense – or austere your room is, how formal or untidy, can have an effect on your counselling relationship. It is probably a transitory effect but may make developing trust and clear communication easier or more difficult. If a client's early impression of you is negative, you will need to work correspondingly hard for that impression to change.

A practical approach, as in marketing, is to ask other people for their views of your room and where it is. More sophisticated, if you wish to see or avoid clients with particular preferences, is to ask people with those preferences for their reactions and what they'd like to be different. However, your own comfort also matters. I remember one of my students (an ENFP) finding the counselling rooms at the university unpleasantly impersonal, so she brought a flower in a small pot each week to put on the table.

Thus, your control of the furniture, decor, location and so on may be very limited but there will be some possibilities. Other features of your room to consider for their effects on your clients and yourself (and preferences will play a part – other ENFPs and Ss seem more likely to warm to the flower and TJs to see it as frivolous) are your clothes, jewellery, any pictures or personal objects and equality of seating (Bayne et al., 2008).

In this chapter, I've discussed several ways in which preference theory may improve the counselling relationship and therefore therapeutic outcomes, for example matching counsellors and clients at different stages of their relationship or different stages of change. The different 'languages' proposed also have implications for attracting, or at least not deterring, clients with different preferences in your advertising materials and by the appearance of your counselling room. In the next chapter, I review first a general model of the preferences and communication and then turn to personality as a factor in explaining, managing and sometimes resolving clients' problems with love and work.

Chapter 5

How Personality Can Affect Clients' Problems with Love and Work

This chapter discusses personality and:

- communication as a general or part solution to some problems with love and work;
- conceptions of love and of ideal romantic partners;
- the role of similarity in romantic relationships;
- being a good parent or guardian;
- looking for work that 'fits' and improving CVs and selection interview 'performance';
- time 'management';
- learning styles;
- being made redundant;
- not speaking in work meetings.

This chapter first builds on some of the ideas about the preferences and communication reviewed in Chapter 4 by outlining a more general model of sources of communication problems between people of opposite preferences. The term 'personality clashes' includes some of these problems, while preference theory implies possible strategies for managing or resolving them. Assertiveness skills such as saying no, making requests and giving and receiving criticisms and compliments are also often useful strategies (Dickson, 1987; Nicolson & Bayne, in press).

The other two sections of the chapter focus on the preferences and examples of problems with love and work respectively. They are organised around questions that clients have asked, and replies to them. They include useful ideas and findings for counselling from the extensive social psychology literature on personality and romantic relationships, including different conceptions of love, likely conflicts between people of different and the same preferences, problems in being a parent or guardian, seeking work, choosing particular kinds of work and shaping and enjoying work.

The replies are potentially relevant in all stages of counselling, though most often as new perspectives. For some of the replies there is direct and substantial research evidence, while others follow directly from preference theory and thus are supported indirectly by the evidence for the theory's validity (discussed in Chapter 1). They are far from conclusive answers; but while much about love and work remains mysterious, psychology is making useful progress.

THE PREFERENCES AND COMMUNICATION: PROBLEMS AND STRATEGIES

Table 5.1 lists the most likely general sources of problems in everyday communication between people with each opposing pair of preferences. For example, Jonathon Rauch wrote about the problem of too much social contact in an article called 'Caring for your introvert' (Rauch, 2003). He described denying (to himself too) that he was an introvert for many years and how liberated he felt when he eventually 'came out'. One way he has cared for himself since is to make sure that he has enough time alone. For him, this is about two hours alone for every hour he's with others. That's rather precise and no one knows the range of amounts of time which different introverts (and most extraverts) ideally need alone and to recover from being sociable or behaving in other E ways.

Introverts' need for so much time alone might well be hard for Es to accept. Conversely, Rauch shows that he doesn't accept an aspect of the preference for E when he comments that Es 'wilt' when they are alone. This is too harsh and too broad a generalisation; it would be true only of people with both highly developed E and little development of I. On the other hand, I agree with Rauch that when Is say to Es, 'I need some time alone, I just want to be quiet for a while', the well-meaning but unhelpful reaction is all too often, 'Are you upset about something?' or 'Would you like us to do something to cheer you up?' The answer is usually no. That's not to say that we don't sometimes feel energised by talking to other

Table 5.1 Opposed preferences and central problems in communication

Pairs of preferences	Associated problems
E versus **I**	Needing contact versus needing time alone
S versus **N**	Giving details and being practical versus emphasising the general picture and speculation
T versus **F**	Being critical and unsympathetic versus illogical and gentle
J versus **P**	Being decisive and needing to plan versus being flexible and easy going
C versus **W**	Being calm and carefree versus worrying and careful

people, rather that we tend to find it more draining than Es and to feel more comfortable and energised when being quiet.

A striking example of the preference for T came in an interview of Jonathan Miller by Laurie Taylor (in the *In Confidence* series, Sky Arts, May 2010). Dr Miller said: 'I was never interested in helping people ... I was entirely, as I always have been about everything in my life, driven by rapacious curiosity. I want to know how things work.' Here he is saying that he loves puzzles, solutions and explanations – and, quite dramatically, that being helpful to people is of no interest at all. He may be overstating this point, not be quite as pure an example of the preference for T as this sounds, but the general implication remains true: that communicating with someone who prefers T is likely to be more effective if you appeal to their curiosity more than their compassion.

Penelope Lively's novel *Spiderweb* includes a pure expression of the preference for J versus P. Two of her characters, young students called Nadine and Stella, are discussing their different approaches to life. Nadine says, 'The thing about life is to have a strategy.' Stella disagrees absolutely: 'The thing about life is to act expediently and creatively. Seize the day. See what comes up and act accordingly.' Nadine proposes a plan – that every five years they check to see who has succeeded the most: 'I chalk up strategic success and you prove opportunistic gains.' From a preference theory point of view, who succeeds most will depend on many other factors – such as how 'success' is defined, luck, and how developed their respective preferences for J and P are – but not on either preference being superior in this respect. Rather, both preferences have strengths and corresponding weaknesses.

Table 5.2 lists general strategies for managing the problems listed in Table 5.1. They are constructive starting points for action or may help clarify whether your client finds it worth trying to solve the particular problem. Specific examples are discussed later in this chapter.

Table 5.2 General ways of managing problems in communicating between people of opposing preferences

Preferences	Strategies
E ⇨ I	Give space. Look for explanations other than 'X doesn't care about me' (e.g., 'X needs to go "inside" to recover from too much extraverting, it's not about me'). Give information before a work meeting.
I ⇨ E	Give attention. Allow time for thinking aloud. Recognise a need for variety of activity. Explain what you as an I need and why, and accept their different need as natural for them.
S ⇨ N	Try adding the N characteristic of beginning with the main point or theme (rather than leading up to it). Ask for ideas. Perhaps also cut some of the detail. But retain your strengths of being realistic, practical etc.
N ⇨ S	Try adding or starting with facts and details. Or say that your idea is only half-formed but there could be something useful there. Select one or two possibilities only at a time.
T ⇨ F	Try adding the F characteristics of (a) saying first what you agree about and (b) the effects on people's emotions, to your analysis. But emphasise your usual strengths of being critical and logical. Share some personal information.
F ⇨ T	Try adding the T characteristics of including reasons and consequences, and being brief. But continue to emphasise impact on people and relevant values – calmly. Be direct and brief.
J ⇨ P	Allow room for flexibility and changes of mind. Recognise that Ps need not to feel controlled. Trust developed Ps to meet deadlines.
P ⇨ J	Allow room for planning and structure. Recognise that Js need to control and the effect of this need on you.
C ⇨ W	Accept that Ws naturally react strongly and, perhaps as a consequence, worry. Recognise that sometimes they have a point.
W ⇨ C	Accept that Cs are easy going and readily take what you see as risks. Recognise that sometimes they are right.

These are general strategies. They are likely therefore to need modifying for particular situations: for example, when making a case to your manager, you may choose to talk more in their language (in the sense discussed in Chapter 4) and less in your own than with you do with a friend. For more on preference theory and communication, see VanSant (2003) and Zeisset (2006).

The four temperaments and communication

Another approach to communication problems that I find useful is the four temperaments model, which was discussed briefly in Chapters 2 and 3. Some clients find the associated stick figures engaging and illuminating, others reject them as too simple or 'pop psychology'. Temperament may influence such judgements! Some implications of the temperament model for improving communication are:

- SPs tend to like action, so if they see a practical problem that they want to do something about, stand aside! They hate feeling trapped, so offer options and avoid pressurising.
- SJs tend to like tradition and structure, so are decisive and orderly, specific and detailed. They tend to focus on a task until it is finished and to dislike distractions. In a workshop, Otto Kroeger advised 'hit and run' when you want to suggest a change of plan to someone who prefers S and J: speak concisely and leave quickly!
- NTs criticise to improve something or someone and analyse with precision, so like debating, solving problems impersonally and using complicated theories to do so. Therefore, offer (well-reasoned) criticism, be prepared to have your competence tested, and try not to take criticism personally. Indeed, it may well be a compliment: your idea is worth bothering with.
- NFs like to develop themselves as people and to help others to do the same. They provide (and need) encouragement, warmth and approval, and they take criticism personally. Their approach is naturally collaborative.

SOME PROBLEMS WITH LOVE

This section and the following section on work are organised around questions which clients sometimes ask and possible responses to them.

Client 1: Love bothers me: how do I know...?

After, of course, helping your client explore and clarify what they mean by this question, you might offer them John Lee's ideas about styles of loving (Lee, 1988; Hendrick & Hendrick, 2008). This model can be a new perspective on the client's worry in its own right, though it is sometimes challenging or threatening too. The preferences are a useful way of making it more acceptable, or at least of making consideration of each style as true love for some people more likely.

Lee's research is based on the results of participants sorting a set of 1500 cards each describing an emotion, action or idea which might occur in a romantic relationship and then being interviewed about their choices. It suggests five main styles of loving plus three main combinations. These styles are briefly defined in Table 5.3, and Lee (1988) provides clear, detailed descriptions of them.

Some links between the preferences and love styles are obvious, for example the idealism of NFs with Eros but not with Storge and Pragma, Ws with Mania, SJs with Storge but not with Eros (fantasy) and Ludus (shallow); and EPs with Ludus. However, such links are only possibilities for a particular client to consider: real people are, of course, more complicated. For example, NTs generally behave unemotionally but, as Keirsey (1988: 242) says, in a defence of this temperament that is fair in my experience, 'powerful passions surge within'.

Lee's positive and accepting approach is very compatible with preference theory. Another model of love, perhaps currently the dominant one in research, is rather more judgemental. Robert Sternberg proposes three components: intimacy, passion and commitment. Combining them gives nine kinds of love, to some of which he gives harsh names, for example 'fatuous love', which is passion plus commitment but not intimacy (Sternberg & Weis, 2006).

Both Lee's and Sternberg's approaches, though, can give clients a clear idea of what's missing or not working, with implications for action. For example, apart from clarifying what love means, clients may discover that

Table 5.3 Eight main styles of loving

Eros	Immediate physical attraction, delight in the other person and a clear physical 'type'
Ludus	Playful, free of commitment and deliberately avoids intensity
Storge	Friendly, companionable and affectionate
Pragma	Practical and realistic – arranged marriages and some approaches to computer dating
Mania	Feverish, obsessive and jealous
Storgic Eros	Friendly intensity
Ludic Eros	Playful intensity
Storgic Ludus	Friendly playfulness

they are drawn to people with a love style they (the client) don't enjoy and perhaps become more able to change this constricting pattern. Lee found that while each of us has a preferred style of love, we can love different partners in different styles or the same partner in different styles at different times.

Lee's model answers many questions about love like, 'Does real love appear suddenly or gradually?' and 'Do I really love her/him?' So, for example, the answer to whether true love appears suddenly or gradually is that it depends: for example, in Eros it's instant and in Storge it's gradual.

Client 2: Which love style is best for me?

Lee found that each combination can work well but that a relationship with someone who has the same love style as your own is more likely to become boring, and that each combination, as well as each style in its own right, has characteristic problems. For example, a Manic lover and a Storgic lover will often misunderstand each other, with accusations from the manic lover of 'You don't love me', and 'If you really loved me ...' And Lee comments that a Manic–Ludic combination is 'bound to be interesting, if not happy' (1988: 54). Indeed, many plays and novels are about the difficulties experienced by this combination of love styles.

Client 3: We kiss so differently...

My client said that his girlfriend finds kissing him too gentle and soft – she describes it, with an affectionate but puzzled smile, as 'like kissing a corpse'. His version was that he likes gentle kissing and that she kisses like a Labrador (said warmly but sadly). They'd shown each other how they'd like to be kissed and smiled about the huge difference but it seemed like an unmovable gap and perhaps one that reflected deeper future problems for them as a couple. He was sad and worried. That he preferred I and she preferred E made their difference easier to accept for a while, but it was not a solution and she ended the relationship.

More generally, preference theory explains, at least in part, some major differences in what people find erotic or a turn-off and it does so without seeing the differences as unnatural or one of them as superior to the other. It suggests that some people really are mismatched and that, as with the authentic chameleon issue discussed in Chapter 4, we vary in how flexible and adaptable we can be or want to be. Other examples of links between the preferences and sex that might cause problems are talking during sex (associated with E), emphasising competence and improvement (T), needing to be 'in the mood' and especially in harmony with our partner (F) and not being taken by surprise (J).

Jones and Sherman (2011) discussed power in love relationships using the metaphor of dances. Among their suggestions for solutions to offer couples with a 'dance problem' are going in two cars to parties for E/I couples and having two televisions for S/N couples: 'People do not need to be glued to each other to belong to each other' (2011: 26).

Client 4: Why do I take so long to recover...?

A possible new perspective would be to explain the client's concern in terms of their style or styles of loving – people who have a Ludic style, for example, tend to recover most quickly and those who have a Manic style least quickly. The most relevant preference is probably W. But in a particular client the influence of each preference may be cumulative (e.g., Mania plus W), or opposed (e.g., Mania versus C) or both (e.g., Mania versus C plus SP) – assuming that Otto Kroeger's view (stated in a workshop), that 'SPs don't hang around dead relationships', is accurate. Other factors which may affect recovery time include the quality and length of the relationship, how surprised or shocked your client is that it ended, the manner of the ending and who ended it (see also the section on loss in Chapter 6).

A note on potential problems between people with the same preferences

Characteristic potential problems are:

- Es can become so involved in activities outside the home that they lose touch with each other.
- Is can avoid talking about a problem so that it festers or they make wrong assumptions about their partner.
- Ss can become very set in their ways (and one or both may get bored).
- Ns can become disappointed because their ideals and expectations are unrealistic.
- Ts can enjoy debate so much that they forget to show appreciation.
- Fs can value harmony at the expense of honesty.
- Js: can be too structured and task focused and may also fight over power.

- Ps can play too much, come up with too many options and not decide or finish things.
- Cs can take poorly judged risks.
- Ws can worry unnecessarily and one or both people may become too much of a 'fusspot' for the other.

In each case the general solution, based on preference theory, is for one or both people to develop their relevant non-preference while remaining true to the strengths of their shared preference.

Client 5: I want a good relationship that lasts...

There have been numerous studies of enduring attraction, using various methods and in a variety of countries and eras with large samples of participants. The studies generally agree that similarity in personality is a good indicator but that high neuroticism (which I've called preference for W) is an exception and is associated with dissatisfaction and divorce (Donnellan et al., 2004; Letzring & Noftle, 2010), and that, translating from Big Five terms, preferences for F, N, J and C predict 'relationship satisfaction' most strongly (Malouff et al., 2010).

Preference for F makes particular sense here: Gottman's dramatic research predicting with 94% accuracy which couples will stay married can be interpreted as showing that extreme T communications (without a modifying F element) are a major risk factor (Gottman, 1994). He found that couples who spoke to each other critically and without warmth – T and little or no F – were far more likely to separate.

More specifically, Gottman distinguished four ways of communicating that predicted divorce: criticism of the partner's personality; contempt/disgust with them, including sarcasm; defensiveness, including making excuses and not taking responsibility; and stonewalling or refusing to respond. This finding does embody some hope because communication skills can be modified and non-preferences can be developed. Elaine Aron's research on the particularly debilitating effect of poor environments on Highly Sensitive People (related to preference for W) is also hopeful because Ws respond particularly well to supportive, respectful environments and relationships.

However, that's a general answer to this client's question – that is, choose someone who prefers F, N, J and C or be very accepting of someone who prefers W – when of course many other factors are involved and there is the further question of similarity of personality.

Here the extensive research clearly supports similarity of personality in some respects as increasing the chances of a high quality and lasting marriage. Rammsted and Schupp (2008), for example, studied nearly 7000 couples and found, translating from Big Five terms, that similarity in F, J and N was strongly related to lasting marriage (and similarity of the opposite preferences, for T, P and S, was associated with divorce). Overall, perhaps the best answer to this client's question is to use preference theory primarily or only to understand and appreciate partners and relationships – and definitely not try to change them into people with the same preferences as yourself!

Client 6: I feel such a bad mother...

Parents and guardians who feel guilty and inadequate can be confused by the complicated and conflicting advice from experts on child rearing. Preference theory's approach is, not surprisingly, that there is no one best way to bring up children, and to treat your child in ways that encourage them to express and therefore develop their preferences. Moreover, it recommends trusting your own instincts and not trying to be a perfect parent.

The myth of the perfect parent is countered positively in Elizabeth Murphy (1992) and by Janet Penley's organisation, M.O.M.S (Mothers Of Many Styles), website, newsletter and book (Penley, with Eble, 2006). Penley's approach is to:

1. Increase self-awareness (for Penley, the eight MBTI preferences).
2. Believe that good mothers come in many styles.
3. Don't covet other mothers' styles.
4. Appreciate yourself first, then the differences in your children, partner and other mothers (including perhaps your own mother).

Some aspects of being a good parent or guardian come naturally for people of each preference, while others are more difficult and draining. For example, respecting a child's privacy and just 'being' with them tends to be more natural for parents who prefer I, encouraging realism more natural for those who prefer S. Each of the ten preferences (adding C and W) has strengths that are valuable in parenting. In marked contrast, mainstream developmental psychology sees some of the Big Five characteristics as related to better quality of parenting (Prinzi et al., 2009).

SOME PROBLEMS WITH WORK

Client 1: What work would suit me?

Many factors are involved in the work a person does (paid or unpaid), including availability, luck, knowing that it exists at all, creating it yourself, contacts, family pressure, media images and personality. Personality does matter: people of different preferences tend to find some occupations and careers more fulfilling than others (Bayne, 2004; Tieger & Barron-Tieger, 2007). However, it is not a simple matching process because people with a variety of preferences can be found in each kind of work.

There are two main outcomes for those who do not use their preferences much more than their non-preferences in their work. The more likely outcome, according to preference theory, is that they will be unhappy and unfulfilled. The second possible outcome is that they will make an unusual and positive contribution because they take a different approach to the majority of their colleagues. It would be interesting to interview the people with unusual preferences for particular occupations – for example, ISFP managers, ESTJ counsellors, INFP accountants – but, except for one study by Jean Kummerow (1998), discussed later in this reply, the research has not been done yet. However, a client who is drawn to an untypical occupation for their preferences might well find it worthwhile to seek out such people.

Temperament theory provides a useful shortcut to the ideas and evidence about careers that are more and less likely to fit each temperament; it is simpler and therefore loses information compared to using all the preferences, but is correspondingly easier to apply. Some of the links between temperament and occupations are as follows:

- SPs tend to be performers, entrepreneurs, one-person businesses and troubleshooters.
- SJs tend to be managers, accountants, police officers, dentists and teachers.
- NTs tend to be scientists, engineers, designers, managers and architects.
- NFs tend to be counsellors, journalists, artists, psychologists and clergy.

Some careers are dominated by a particular temperament: for example, in large samples, over half of clergy and counsellors are NFs, compared with only 4% of farmers and the police (Myers & McCaulley, 1985). This is even more striking when the proportion of NFs in the general population is taken into account. In the UK it is 14% and in the USA 16% (from general population samples; method and data discussed in Bayne, 2004). General population UK and US figures for the other temperaments are: SPs 27% and 25% respectively, SJs 51% and 43%, and NTs 9% and 10%.

In mainstream occupational psychology, the Big Five characteristic of conscientiousness is seen as particularly important in selection for jobs. The consensus (stated, as it usually is, in strong terms) is that 'Individuals who are dependable, persistent, goal directed and organised tend to be higher performers on virtually any job' (Mount & Barrick, 1998: 851). In this quote Mount and Barrick are describing people with a preference for J. Their view of people with a preference for P is that 'Those who are careless, irresponsible, low achievement, striving and impulsive tend to be lower performers on virtually any job' (p. 851). Thus, for them, the practical implication is clear: 'No matter what job you are selecting for, if you want employees to be good performers, you should hire those who work smarter and work harder' (p. 856).

The preference theory view of preference for P or low conscientiousness is radically different. It is that organisations that follow Mount and Barrick's advice, which is still the consensus in occupational psychology in 2012, will miss the typical strengths of Ps such as their flexibility and the troubleshooting, calmness and practical intelligence of SPs. However, such organisations may be saved to some extent by the imperfections of selection procedures and the ability of applicants to edit their self-presentations!

In addition, there is a clear positive relationship between preference for C and highly dangerous occupations like bomb disposal and guarding VIPs (Glicksohn & Rechtman, 2011). Careers which are more frequently chosen by Ws include strategists, advisers, healers, law interpreters and artists (Aron, 2010).

Moreover, as mentioned above, many jobs can be done effectively in very different ways. For example, scientists can be detectives, classifiers, visionaries etc. A study by Jean Kummerow (1998) illustrates this fact well and more studies of this kind would be very useful. She interviewed a librarian of each of the 16 MBTI types (finding them was an achievement in itself) about the aspects of their work which they particularly enjoyed. Each had found a niche or specialism that suited their preferences. For example, the ESTP said that 'being away from her desk' and 'adapting technologies to the library's needs' were what appealed to her; the INTJ that it was 'developing and working with policies'; and the INFP 'forming personal relationships with customers and enjoying their idiosyncrasies' (1998: 302).

At the same time, different occupations do tend to suit people with different preferences, as shown clearly, systematically and in detail by Paul Tieger and Barbara Barron-Tieger in their book on the MBTI preferences and career choice (Tieger & Barron-Tieger, 2007). For example, they see ISFPs as flourishing most when their work is consistent with their values, is in a supportive and affirming environment, involves attending to detail and working with real things that benefit other people, allows the freedom to work independently but with other 'compatible and courteous' people nearby, and allows them to use their sense of aesthetics to enhance their place of work. Tieger and Barron-Tieger discuss the most and least popular careers for each 'type' and characteristic strengths and weaknesses in searching for work.

Client 2: How can I improve my CV?

Finding a fulfilling career often involves selling yourself, which appeals much more to people with some sets of preferences than others. Preference theory can help by explaining any distaste in a positive way and through using parts of the descriptions of the preferences to communicate your strengths. The strengths questionnaires discussed in Chapter 3 can also contribute. A good CV describes activities and achievements that show your preferences and strengths in action and *specifically* (which is an S skill). For example, not 'Team player' but 'Played X for Y years ... and we ...'. And not 'Experienced in writing client reports' but 'Wrote six reports averaging 1000 words a week for ... on ... analysing ...'. Other words that are overused and, without specific examples, empty, include 'creative', 'visionary', 'leadership', 'communication skills' etc.

Client 3: How can I improve my interview technique?

As in the previous answer about improving CVs, plus practice with skilful, constructive feedback (Bayne, 2004). Listen to the interviewer's questions and 'language' (in the sense used in Chapter 4).

Client 4: I've been late too often...

Preference theory contributes a more varied view of time than the standard one in time management courses, books and articles. For example, the courses are usually heavily biased towards a J approach and thus tend to leave Ps unchanged or demoralised. They may also affect some people with a preference for J adversely by encouraging them to be *too* organised – to the point of obsession.

People with a preference for P do not see time as something you manage; rather, it flows. The practical implication of this is that techniques like planning ahead in detail are actually counterproductive for the large proportion (about 45%) of the UK and USA who prefer P. (See Table 5.4 for some non-standard techniques.)

The difference between Js' and Ps' relationship with time seems to be based on different basic motives: to control and organise versus to adapt and be flexible. The starting position of Js is that free time is what's left over after planned activities have been completed, while for Ps, time is free, except for what's planned.

Both approaches to time have potential problems. For example, Js may complete something even though it's become irrelevant, and they may find it difficult or impossible to relax. Potential problems for Ps include being criticised by Js for not planning and for leaving things to the last minute, and some tasks being too complicated to do at the last minute. Developed Ps learn how to time tasks and split them up into sub-tasks, each with their own energising deadline. Clashes between Js and Ps at work and elsewhere seem to be common.

A subtle problem can occur when one person tries to help someone of the opposite preference by themselves behaving out of preference. For example, a J behaves more spontaneously and flexibly with a P colleague than she (the person who prefers J) is comfortable with and the P colleague says, 'That was great, I really enjoyed working with you and look forward to our next project.' She or he may mean well but is not respecting (or may not be aware of) the different style of the colleague with the preference for J. In addition, the J is both not using her strengths as much as she might *and* being encouraged to neglect them again. However, whether this is a problem is a matter of degree, self-monitoring, judgement and assertiveness. If the person adapting is enjoying developing their non-preference, it isn't a problem (at least not short term) but if they feel trapped, it is.

A note on time 'management'

Table 5.4 lists some other ways of managing time for people with the different combinations of the preferences for S, N, J and P.

Table 5.4 Four pairs of preferences and time

SJs	Timetables and calendars Lists which are specific, worked through systematically and checked off each day
SPs	Work on whatever is needed at that moment Find ways to make the work fun
NJs	Lists as overviews, to see what there is to do at some point, including long term, e.g., years ahead Natural planners who work in bursts
NPs	Many projects at a time and at different stages Life unfolds and things get done, usually with some help from increased energy at the last minute Work best from inspiration, not according to plans

Table 5.5 Eight preferences and aspects of learning styles associated with them

E	Action, talk, trial and error, breadth
I	Reflection, working privately, depth
S	Focusing closely on what is actually happening or actually there, theory later
N	Theory first, possibilities, surges of interest
T	Analysis, logic, critiques, objectivity
F	Harmonious atmosphere, need to care about the topic
J	Organised, formal, clear expectations; work first, play later
P	Work is play, flexible, bursts of energy, work in different rooms, find your natural rhythm

Client 5: We have a new trainer and I can't follow him at all...

Aspects of the learning styles associated with each of the MBTI preferences are listed in Table 5.5. For example, brainstorming is as natural as breathing for people with some preferences, but pointless or even threatening to others. It's inevitable, though, that trainees' preferred learning style or styles will not always match those of trainers. That seems to be happening here – it sounds as though this client may prefer S and his new trainer may prefer N and thus hasn't developed, or at least does not use, the S skills of being specific and concrete.

The difference between preferring S and N is seen as a 'chasm' by some leading authorities on the MBTI. For example, Chuck Pratt in a 1999 conference paper said it was 'the biggest source of conflict in the workplace', with the most potential for conflict and loss of productivity, while Mary McCaulley (1996) recommended that Ss appreciate how agonising it is for Ns to 'spell out our great ideas step by step' and that Ns recognise that Ss find it fun to make ideas practical and useful (see Table 5.2). For more on the preferences and learning styles, see John DiTiberio and Allen Hammer (1993) and Gordon Lawrence (1997).

Client 6: I've been made redundant and I'm struggling...

If you think your client prefers F, preference theory suggests that you respond warmly and empathically first and wait for your client to feel ready to clarify what 'struggling' means and perhaps check what they've tried that hasn't helped, or hasn't helped enough. If your judgement that your client prefers F seems wrong or your initial judgement is that your client prefers T, then be briefly empathic and quite quickly more business-like and focused on problem solving. She or he may express emotions more in due course. A possible next step is discussed in the section on loss in Chapter 6.

Client 7: I rarely speak in meetings...

Your client probably prefers I and hasn't developed his E skills in this respect, or there may be something about the particular meetings. Encouraging him to 'jump in' – to just do it – probably won't help. Preference theory suggests some system change. Thus, your client could ask for more detailed information about the topics before meetings and, in the meetings themselves, for 'thinking time' and/or brief discussions in pairs which report back to the meeting. The last two suggestions are more novel and perhaps open to ridicule but the general argument for them is a strong one: organisations benefit from using the different strengths of all their staff. You may also want to explore and challenge the hint of 'preference envy' (in this case of Es) in this client's way of presenting his problem.

In this chapter, I've discussed preference theory and communication problems and strategies with love and work, for example with different styles of loving and approaches to time 'management' respectively. In the next chapter, I turn to personality as a valuable perspective on clients' problems with aspects of physical and mental health.

Chapter 6

How Personality Can Affect Clients' Problems with Health

This chapter discusses personality and:

- physical and mental health;
- managing stress;
- losing weight;
- exercise;
- personality disorders;
- ADHD and ADD;
- dementia.

This chapter is in three parts: an introduction to personality applied to physical and mental health; a section on problems in physical health structured, like Chapter 5, as responses to statements by clients; and notes on problems in mental health. Both the second and third sections illustrate the potential relevance of preference theory including core motives, and occasionally integrative life stories, to counselling clients with a variety of health problems. The section on mental health is structured differently because I am not an expert in psychiatry or psychopathology and my experience as a counsellor is mainly non-clinical. In this section, I give examples of the different perspective of preference theory compared with mainstream clinical psychology and psychiatry on personality disorders, ADHD and dementia.

All counsellors, whatever their training, are likely to have clients with serious mental health problems and those clients' reactions to labels such as 'personality disorder' and 'schizophrenia' can be usefully discussed with them. They can also be helped to develop ways of coping (Joseph & Linley, 2006), with the counsellor working in a supportive way and the client seeing a specialist as well. Susy Churchill (2011) reviews psychiatric classifications and practice guidelines in detail. The website www.mentalhealthcare.org.uk is an evidence-based website on myths and misinformation about psychosis, treatments and mental health services.

In physical health, relationships between personality and longevity were touched on in Chapter 1. However, generally the relationship between personality and particular illnesses is not strong (an exception is hostility, an element of low Agreeableness or preference for T, and heart disease; Wiebe et al. 2010). Moreover, many health problems and their relationship to personality are generally not well understood despite considerable progress (e.g., Lahey, 2009; French et al., 2010).

Therefore, I focus on the preferences and three relatively straightforward health problems: ways of coping with stress, reducing weight and increasing exercise.

Chronic stress, obesity and inactivity are major public health problems in Western society and thus enormously costly to countries' economies and to individuals' well-being. They also increase the risk of several major mental and physical illnesses (French et al., 2010).

The stages of change model discussed in Chapter 4 is potentially very useful in helping clients cope better with stress, sustain weight loss and increase activity. In addition, some recent research in health psychology is consistent with and may enhance the action stage of widely used approaches to integrative counselling. For example, the amount of walking is substantially increased by changing a belief that there isn't enough time to do it (Darker et al., 2010). Darker and colleagues showed that asking people to think of times when they found it easy to walk, and what factors made it easier to increase how much they walked, helped them develop concrete plans which they then acted on. This technique will be familiar to many counsellors as force-field analysis (e.g., Bayne et al., 2008).

The large positive effects found by Darker et al. were maintained in the six-week follow-up period, and their research group is continuing to evaluate, develop and extend the technique to specific groups, such as those who have recently had a stroke (Williams & French, 2011). Other researchers have shown the positive effects of brisk walking (getting slightly out of breath) on physical and mental health. Inactivity is a cause of obesity and other serious illnesses, while exercise is an effective way of helping prevent and treat them (Biddle, 2010); and a new and valuable finding is that avoiding continuous sitting for long periods, say for more than half an hour, is also healthier (Biddle, 2010).

Preference theory adds to these useful and strong general findings in two ways. First, health promotion campaigns seem likely to be more effective if they target people with certain personality characteristics. For example, preferences for E and P (translating from Big Five terms) were found to be associated with obesity and weight gain by Magee and Heaven (2011) in a study of over 5000 Australian adults for two years, and by Sutin et al. (2011), analysing data from over 1900 participants in a longitudinal study of more than 50 years. Preferences for F and W may be further risk factors.

People who prefer both E and P seek novelty and drama and are likely to ignore a campaign which lacks these qualities. Moreover, their ideas about what counts as dramatic will be different from the ideas of people with opposing preferences, and they should therefore be involved in designing the campaigns directed at them. Second, it suggests fundamental links between personality and the kinds of exercise which are enjoyable or repugnant (see reply to Client 2 below) and which they are therefore correspondingly more or less likely to continue with.

PHYSICAL HEALTH

Client 1: I'm tired all the time...

Being tired all the time is a classic symptom of too much stress – but it can also be a symptom of several illnesses, so your client may need to see their GP. Clarifying possible causes of chronic stress is another possibility, and preference theory states that the activities and circumstances which are enjoyable for people with some preferences are stressful for those with the opposite preferences. Table 6.1 illustrates this idea for the ten preferences. The causes of stress, reactions to it (Table 6.2) and coping methods that work and don't work (Table 6.3) are clues to your client's preferences and their non-preferences as well. At the least, reviewing these tables with your client can open up options to try out and increase their sense of hope and control (Nicolson & Bayne, in press).

A further prediction from preference theory is the varying reactions to too much stress of people with different preferences. Here I find temperament a useful model (see Table 6.2).

Table 6.3 suggests different coping methods for people with each preference. They are a mix of problem-solving and distraction techniques. The underlying principle is to use your own preferences as a first attempt at

Table 6.1 The preferences and what tends to be experienced as particularly stressful

E	Not much happening; not enough contact with people
I	Not enough time for reflection or for oneself
S	Vagueness and abstract theory
N	Routine, repetitive and detailed activities
T	Lack of logic, intense emotions
F	Conflict and criticism, discourtesy
J	Lack of plans and changes of plan
P	Restrictions on autonomy, few or no options
C	Not much! People with this preference 'really are calm and untroubled' (Miller, 1991: 422).
W	Conflict, disappointments, upsets

Table 6.2 The four temperaments and reactions to stress

SP	Flight, frivolity, breakdown
SJ	Dogmatic, more effort, more attempt to control
NT	Overwork, fight, conform rebelliously
NF	Hysteria, cynicism, self-sacrifice

coping. This happens naturally if the preference is sufficiently developed and circumstances allow. If these methods don't work, Kroeger et al. (2002: 252–3) suggest a 'good stretch', by which they mean a *brief* switch to using your non-preferences. Obviously, such a formulation risks being attacked for 'having it both ways'; however, the emphasis on being brief and the sequence of trying the two kinds of strategy is a good counter-argument. A good stretch is also a 'rest' for your natural ways of coping. In Table 6.3, the source of stress is referred to as X.

A note on stress

Another perspective on the preferences and coping with stress comes from a study of interactions between combinations of (translating from Big Five terms) EI, JP and CW, giving eight personality types (Vollrath & Torgersen, 2000). Nearly 700 participants reported on their daily hassles, positive and negative emotions and coping strategies. Not surprisingly, JCs reported the least stress and most effective coping, PWs the most stress and poor coping. This typology (Table 6.4) deserves further study, for example, of which coping techniques work best and least for each of the types.

Table 6.3 The preferences and ways of coping with stress

Preference	To try first	A 'good stretch'
E	Talking about X	Quiet reflection, perhaps through writing, about X
I	Quiet reflection about X	Talking freely about X
S	Any practical activity requiring concentration	Any imaginative or creative activity
N	Design something	Do something practical and detailed
T	Analyse X or something else	Empathise with someone connected to X (if there is someone else involved), try to see and feel from their point of view
F	Empathise or create/find harmony	Analyse X or something else
J	Make a plan or finish a task	Behave spontaneously (for a few minutes?)
P	Do something you feel like doing at a pace that suits you	Make a plan and carry it out (for a few minutes?)
C	Stay calm	Make a list of worries and threats, however absurd and unlikely they seem, and think of ways to reduce risk
W	Consider more precautions to further reduce worries and threats	Try mindfulness, slow, deep breathing or other ways of reducing worry

Source: Adapted from Kroeger et al. (2002: 253).

Clearly, Vollrath and Torgersen's language is much less positive and even-handed than preference theory, but it does suggest aspects to work on with clients of each set of preferences to reduce their stress. The combination of W and P is, as they found, particularly vulnerable to stress, and Miller (1991) calls I, W and P (again translating from Big Five terms) the 'misery triad' and sees those who have these characteristics as apparently having 'little capacity for well-being' (1991: 430). However, my experience is different and I think Aron's much more positive ideas and findings about Highly Sensitive People are a very important alternative view, as discussed in Chapters 1 and 4.

At present quite a lot is known about generally effective methods of coping with stress – exercise, sleep, expressive writing, music and so forth (Nicolson & Bayne, in press) – but the best approach to finding optimum coping methods may be for each client to experiment for themselves using preference theory to guide *what* they try and *how* they approach it. The

Table 6.4 Personality characteristics associated with eight sets of preferences

Sets of preferences	Name	Some characteristics
I, C, P	Spectator	Emotionally flat, not ambitious, not very interested in social norms
I, W, P	Insecure	Very sensitive to own physical and mental experiences, dependent on other people's opinions, poorly organised
I, C, J	Sceptic	Self-controlled, somewhat rigid, emotionally stable
I, W, J	Brooding	Shy, tend to give up easily, very scrupulous
E, C, P	Hedonist	Pleasure-orientated, robust physically and emotionally, undependable, socially skilled
E, W, P	Impulsive	Pleasure-oriented, attention seeking, emotional outbursts
E, C, J	Entrepreneur	Socially secure, little control over emotions, independent, domineering, goal orientated
E, W, J	Complicated	Emotionally intense, organised, dependent on others

Source: Adapted from Vollrath and Torgersen (2000: 368–9) and preferences substituted for Big Five terms.

same general strategy applies to reducing or stopping smoking, drinking too much alcohol and other addictions.

Client 2: I want to lose weight and I've tried so many different ways...

Timothy Miller's client who hated herself for being overweight was briefly discussed in Chapter 4. Her personality included being low on conscientiousness (the parallel of preferring P plus not having developed her non-preference for J very much) and Miller attributed her non-compliance with standard techniques, like calorie counting (despite his 'continuing encouragement' she didn't buy a counter) and keeping a diary of what she ate, as an effect of her core personality – not resistance – and something that was very unlikely to change. With other clients who preferred P and who had other problems, he tried 'interpretation, confrontation, treatment contracts, paradoxical approaches, self-monitoring and other methods with little apparent success' (1991: 430). It's therefore not surprising that

Miller sees psychotherapy as just not working with such clients (1991, as also discussed in Chapter 4).)

Preference theory is more optimistic. It offers a set of strategies that Miller didn't consider, and a rationale for who to use them with. Thus, because people with a marked preference for P tend to resent rules and plans, they find it easier to go on what Susan Scanlon (1986) calls a 'sort of diet'. She suggested strategies for each of the four temperaments and Table 6.5 summarises these. It is quite specific, but speculative and incomplete, and the main point is that different strategies seem likely to be effective for clients with different preferences, or at the very least are likely to be worth discussing with them first. In addition, it suggests which strategies are likely to be futile or counterproductive for each temperament.

By 'sort of diet' (for SPs and perhaps NPs too), Scanlon means lots of variety and flexibility, therefore stocking up with healthy and mainly low calorie food and enjoying choosing just before eating while trying to eat a bit less than usual. It also means not keeping many high calorie foods within easy reach, because Ps tend to have poor impulse control. Conversely, planning meals a week ahead, measuring portions and keeping records all appeal to SJs' discipline and sense of responsibility.

Another strategy, one that uses S, N, T and F, is as follows:

1. Use S to ask 'Am I really hungry?' If not, 'What is it about this situation that makes me want to eat? Is it for comfort, out of boredom, to avoid a particular emotion, to please somebody …?

Table 6.5 The four temperaments and losing weight

Temperament	Strategy
SP	Use or develop their natural strength of being in touch with feeling hungry and with when they are full. Refine this to judging what *exactly* it is that they want to eat. Make dieting as much fun as possible and don't plan. Focus on the process, not on goals.
SJ	Plan meals and times. Use their natural strengths of being strong-willed, organised and task focused.
NT	Like to know theory and to design their own variations of diets. Want reasons and evidence.
NF	Need to find a personal meaning for losing weight, such as doing it for someone else. Will diet when it feels right and are likely to diet in bursts.

Source: Adapted from Kroeger (1985) and Scanlon (1986).

2. Use N to imagine other causes and other ways of meeting the particular need.
3. Use T to come up with the arguments for and against each possible action.
4. Use F to apply whichever core value or values are relevant and to include effects on other people of each action.

The general approach of preference theory to losing weight is therefore to raise awareness that standard techniques tend to suit people with the SJ temperament; to suggest alternative techniques which are better suited to people with the other temperaments; and possibly to help them develop their non-preferences a little (but less than their preferences). For example, developing the S ability to be very sensitive to how they are feeling physically is possible for NTs and NFs but, according to preference and temperament theory, much more difficult for them to do.

Big Five theory and research sometimes clashes with preference theory and sometimes agrees with it. As before, the preference for P is the main contrast. For example, Sutin et al. (2011: 589) wrote that, 'Individuals high on impulsivity and low on Conscientiousness may benefit most from interventions that stress menu planning and regular meal schedules' – the opposite recommendation to preference theory. On the other hand, their second strategy of group settings for Es is consistent with preference theory.

Client 3: I know I need to do more exercise but it's so boring...

Suzanne Brue has studied the relationships between the preferences and how people enjoy exercise for many years. Her book summarises data from interviews and questionnaires which produced 'bold patterns' (Brue, 2008: 17). For example, people who prefer I, N and J tend to enjoy exercising alone in a calm, familiar and pleasing setting and letting their minds drift – exercise as a 'moving meditation' – whereas people who prefer E, S and P tend to enjoy lots of stimulation, variety and quick responding – exercise as absorbing action. As these examples suggest, the key variables may be motives, with the actual form of exercise a way of fulfilling them and increased health a side effect. Table 6.6 summarises some of her main findings. For rationales, examples, subtle points and tips, see Brue (2008) and her website: www.suzannebrue.com. Partial rationales are included in the table.

Brue ends her book with tips for coaching people with each of the sets of preferences. Whatever exercise you choose, standard and justified precautions are to increase its length and intensity comfortably and

Table 6.6 Eight sets of preferences and favourite kinds of exercise

Preferences	Form of exercise	Aspects of rationale
I, S, J	Cardiovascular, rowing, running, swimming, canoeing, walking, weight training	Familiar routine, easy to keep a record of progress, tradition
E, S, J	Cardiovascular, golf and tennis, running, swimming, walking, yoga	Respectability, keeping a record of progress, structure, experiencing nature, tradition
E, S, P	Basketball, biking, hiking and climbing, in-line skating, racquetball, skiing, tennis	Fun, with others, mini-goals, outdoors, split-second timing, intense
I, S, P	Activities of daily living, biking, hiking, climbing, horse riding, running, skiing, swimming, walking, wind surfing	Alone or with one or two quiet friends, grooming the horse, varied scenery, connection to nature and sensory experience
E, N, P	Biking, cardiovascular, fitness classes, dancing, hiking, running, skiing, yoga and tai chi	Enjoying outdoors, convenience, variety, flair for drama, love of performance, efficiency and fun
I, N, P	Biking, cardiovascular, fitness classes, dance, hiking, martial arts, running, walking and yoga	Outdoors, flow and concentration, self-expression, efficiency and flexibility
I, N, J	Biking, cardiovascular, hiking, strength training, tai chi, walking, yoga	Not social, looking for peace and a respite from the world and efficiency
E, N, J	Biking, cardiovascular, Pilates, running, strength training, swimming, walking and yoga	Measuring progress, variety and flexibility, structured and organised

gradually, and, if you're not used to that form of exercise, to check with your GP or a qualified coach or trainer before doing it.

Client 4: I've got Parkinson's...

A person's preferences affect how they'd rather receive 'bad news', their reactions to it, and how they adapt. Judy Allen and Susan Brock's research (2000) suggests that we would rather receive the bad news in our own 'language' of ST, SF, NT or NF (see Chapter 4), while our reactions and how we subsequently adapt seem likely to be related to our reactions to stress and ways of coping with it (Tables 6.2 and 6.3), combined with relevant elements of loss.

Ron Penner used preference theory with his ME (Chronic Fatigue Syndrome) patients in a support group to help them cope and adjust (Penner, 1992). He found the preferences for J and P particularly helpful. Js found the loss of control and consequent need to slow down particularly challenging – those who adapted better said they had to 'shift gears', which I interpret as developing their non-preference for P a little. In the same way, the Ps who improved said that they added more structure and routine to their daily lives because they had to take more note of what their bodies needed. This is a good example of tailoring information to people with different preferences.

Penner also found temperament theory useful in discussions with his patients. In line with the theory, he found that SPs tended to focus on (worry about) reduced physical capabilities, like their coordination and balance; SJs on their reduced ability to meet their responsibilities and duties; NTs on their sense of competence, on cognitive changes and on what was causing their symptoms; and NFs about the future and the impact of their illness on their loved ones (1992: 16). Thus, he advocated some development of non-preferences for J or P respectively and taking account of the core needs of each of the four temperaments.

A note on loss

Loss is, of course, a frequent theme in counselling: bereavement, being made redundant, the end of a relationship, loss of property, youth and so on. Positive changes can also involve loss. The great variability in people's reaction to loss is related to several characteristics of the loss, such as how it happens, your previous experience of loss, your circumstances and aspects of your personality. According to Wortman and Silver (1989) about 50% of people do not experience intense anxiety, depression or grief after a major loss, and they are not repressing their feelings – a high proportion of them seem likely to prefer C; 30% do experience grief etc. and then recover; 18% are 'chronic grievers'; and 2% seem unaffected at first but within a year or so are distressed.

As Wortman and Silver argue, it follows that needing to 'work through' grief is a myth for many people, and those people are not being callous or insensitive when they adjust relatively easily. Later research, for example Bonanno (2011), similarly shows that for most of us grief is not overwhelming or unending – though that is not to criticise those people for whom it is.

Worden (2008) suggested four 'tasks' of mourning that can be readily adapted to coping with loss generally. They are paraphrased below as:

1. Accept the reality of the loss. Check for denial or minimising.
2. Experience the emotions associated with the loss, such as sadness, happiness, anger, relief, betrayal, regret.
3. Adjust to your new circumstances as much as you wish to and can.
4. Find a 'place' in your thoughts and feelings for the loss if you wish to and can.

These tasks overlap and each may vary in ease for people of different preferences. Each task may be returned to several times and reviewing them can help your client identify what they might still work on.

Whitemore and Dixon (2008) formulated a similar general model of loss on the basis of their research with adults who have a chronic illness. Specifically, they interviewed their participants about how they integrated their illness and their lives. The resulting themes included 'shifting sands', 'staying afloat', 'weathering the storms', 'rescuing oneself' and 'navigating life'. 'Shifting sands' refers to one person's initial response to their diagnosis – she said, 'I felt like I was standing on a sandbar and the sand was washing out beneath my feet …' (2008: 181). I find this a vivid image but I imagine some people would not, and indeed other participants, grouped under the same theme, gave very different responses, for example talking specifically about things they could not do now that they could do before. The two kinds of reaction have an N and S flavour respectively and preference theory could add a new layer of understanding and practice to this model.

MENTAL HEALTH

A note on personality disorders

The term 'personality disorder' is controversial. Do people who are labelled in this way have extreme versions of normal personality characteristics, or are they ill? (Funder, 2010; Widiger & Costa, in press). If they are not ill, a self-actualisation or growth model is appropriate rather than a medical one. Sophia Dunn, a clinical psychotherapist with extensive experience of using the MBTI with clients diagnosed as having a personality disorder, provided dramatic though anecdotal support for the self-actualisation model with these clients (Dunn, 2006).

It is dramatic in part because using a personality questionnaire with people whose personality is 'disordered' seems futile, yet Dunn finds that she is able to use her clients' preferences to understand their particular disorder and to modify her interventions and approach. She sees her clients as having extreme development or non-development of a preference rather than a personality disorder.

For example, she asked an INTP, diagnosed as having a 'schizoid personality disorder', about what interested her most rather than about her presenting problem of lack of close relationships. Further sessions focused on exploring ways of developing the strengths of her preferences and clarifying what had hindered their development. The descriptions of her preferences and psychological type gave this client a glimpse of how she could be at her best, acceptance of that 'kind of person' and a new and positive perspective on what had gone wrong in her life and on why she had been referred to a clinical psychotherapist. It also focused on her as a person with a problem rather than on the problem itself or the problem as a symptom of an illness.

Dunn usually introduces the idea of taking the MBTI carefully and kindly in the first session and her clients complete it in their second session. The setting and timing is important; clients need to feel safe, calm and 'themselves'. Dunn calls these periods 'lulls', and she finds few clients with a diagnosis of personality disorder who are constantly disordered and therefore unable to answer the questionnaire in a meaningful way. She also finds strong consistency between MBTI results from early in her work with the client and at the end of that work (Dunn, 2006).

A note on ADHD and ADD

ADHD (Attention Deficit Hyperactivity Disorder) and ADD (Attention Deficit Disorder) are vague and controversial terms. At their most positive, they attempt to diagnose behaviour interpreted as an illness with a view to treating it and healing or at least managing it; at worst, they are a convenient way of explaining the behaviour of 'difficult' children and justifying controlling them with powerful drugs. Temperament theory suggests that at least some of the children diagnosed with ADHD and ADD have a normal temperament but are in a setting which does not suit them. Their short attention span, crying and laughing a lot and being easily bored and disruptive is for them a normal response to sitting quietly most of the day or studying things that don't interest them. They need a different setting.

The particular temperament is SP. SPs, especially ESPs, want excitement, action and fun *now* and this temperament, although obviously not valued in a diagnosis of ADHD or ADD, is valued by society for some careers and activities (Keirsey, 1998). Descriptions of ENTPs, ENFPs and Ws also overlap considerably with those of people with ADHD and ADD. For example, ENPs tend to start something enthusiastically, then lose interest and become enthusiastic about something else, while Ws may react to being overstimulated by being 'hyper' or unable to focus. Overall, preference theory suggests that people with some preferences (and undeveloped non-preferences) are at risk of being misdiagnosed as having a mental disorder.

Moreover, the strengths of some people diagnosed as having ADHD or ADD are being neglected, as has also been argued for Asperger's syndrome (Chester, 2006; Elliman, 2011) and dyslexia (Grande & Bayne, 2006). For example, adults with ADHD perform better on some measures of creativity and creative achievement than adults without ADHD (White & Shah, 2011). Similarly, Sabina Dosani writes about the evolutionary advantages of ADHD and gives 'sales, politics, entertainment and emergency work' as examples of the kinds of job that allow people with ADHD to 'build on their strengths' (Dosani, 2012: 25).

The National Institute for Health and Clinical Excellence (NICE) website (nice.org.uk) has free guidelines on diagnosing and managing ADD and ADHD which currently (2012) seem to be moving a little in this direction, in particular stressing social and psychological interventions for young children.

A note on dementia

Dementia shows us, very sadly and starkly, how much memories are part of personality. As they slip away, so our sense of self collapses. Dementia is often described as a cruel and terrifying illness with voluntary euthanasia much preferred. However, it is also a gradual process and there is a role (an increasing one if the forecasted increase in numbers of people with dementia is accurate) for counsellors and carers of people with dementia in its early and middle stages (Weakes et al., 2006). This role can include using music, photos, talking, writing and the life story techniques discussed in Chapter 8.

Such interventions have the potential to keep the person with dementia's sense of self relatively alive and intact for longer, to help them understand more and thus be more able to live as 'an active and interactive being operating within a social context' (Cheston & Bender, 2003: 17). Preference theory predicts that the activities which people will, for the most part, find most fulfilling and healthy will be those which use their preferences.

Some researchers are working on which aspects of autobiographical memories and which interventions are most critical for promoting and sustaining well-being (Jetten et al., 2010; Haslam et al., 2011; see also Lee & Adams, 2011). Cathy Haslam and her colleagues argue that findings from several studies with elderly care home residents show that identity strength is a better predictor of well-being than severity of cognitive impairment.

In this chapter, I've illustrated the potential relevance of contemporary personality theory to helping clients manage their problems with physical and mental health, for example losing weight and increasing exercise, and personality disorders and dementia. In the next chapter I return to applications of preference theory to self-awareness with two extended case studies. In the first, Jean Kummerow (ESTJ) reviews her own development in terms of classical psychological type theory, while in the second I review my own development (INFPC) in terms of the variation of preference theory central to this book.

Chapter 7

Extended Case Studies of Personality Development

The case studies in this chapter complement each other in two ways. They are by two people (writing about themselves) who are of opposite preferences in classical MBTI theory: Jean Kummerow's account of her development as an ESTJ illustrates preference theory and two other levels of MBTI theory (type dynamics and function-attitudes), while my account of being an INFPC illustrates the variation of preference theory used most in this book. In addition, you may wish to compare the writing styles: are they different and do they give clues to the writers' preferences? Indirectly, these case studies also introduce the final chapter on integrative life stories; they imply the question of what more the methods of discovering life stories, and possibly reinterpreting them, discussed in that chapter, would add to our self-awareness.

I've used type dynamics only occasionally in this book and function-attitudes not at all. My reasons are that preference theory is both much better supported empirically and simpler (and in my view more useful) to apply, as discussed in Chapter 1 and in Bayne (2005). However, Jean's analysis illustrates preference theory beautifully in content and style and at the same time introduces these other levels of MBTI theory.

Although Jean's analysis can be read and enjoyed without any understanding of the detail of type dynamics and function-attitudes (Myers, K. & Kirby, 1994), the following outline of them may be helpful. She uses the following terms from type dynamics, which is a theory about the structure of personality:

- *Dominant function*, which is in effect the managing director of the personality. It is one of four preferences, those for S, N, T or F. For ESTJs, it is T.

- *Auxiliary function*, which is the second in command. For ESTJs, it is S.
- *Tertiary function*, which is the non-preference opposing the auxiliary function. For ESTJs, it is N.
- *Inferior* or *fourth function*, which is the non-preference opposing the dominant function. For ESTJs, it is F.

The function-attitudes model distinguishes between extraverted and introverted versions of S, N, T and F (Thompson, 1996): for example, Jean writes about her dominant function of 'extraverted Thinking'.

TYPE DEVELOPMENT FROM AN ESTJ PERSPECTIVE, BY JEAN KUMMEROW

This account was based originally on a panel presentation on type development at the International Association for Psychological Type Conference in June 1985. I was in my mid-thirties at the time. Since then, Rowan has asked to reproduce it on three separate occasions, each about a decade apart. And each time, I find myself adding to my understanding of my functions, especially my third and fourth ones (with my first ones needing less editing). I hope this indicates type development.

To put this in context, the first version was a panel, mostly of Intuitive types, and the audience was overwhelmingly Intuitive; I was the only representative of the ST column and the ES quadrant. Thus, I felt a great responsibility to represent not only my type well, but also the other type combinations. Given that most people using this theoretically based instrument are Intuitives, this responsibility continues to today.

As you might guess, I consider responsibility to be a key point in understanding ESTJs. What I say I will do, I will do, and I will try to do it as efficiently as possible, of course. It is almost as if I have made a sacred oath when I agree to do something – when I say it out loud to others, I mean it. As a child, I felt responsible to do things right. I would spend untold hours making sure my school assignments were complete and on time. I could not understand people who would not follow through. In my own critical (and naive) way, I would assume they were either liars who deliberately broke their promises or they were dumb because they forgot their promises. You will be glad to hear I have learned much more understanding and forgiveness since then.

I suppose the question with ESTJs really becomes: what are they responsible for? The first responsibility, quite frankly, is to get the job done properly. We would rather not talk about it; we would rather do it. Of course, part of our type development is learning to value the process or way a job is to be done and that means, too, the people involved, along with the actual completion of the job. One of my favourite tasks in life is to help NPs get organised and off dead centre through encouraging them to move ideas to implementation.

You may have heard me say the word 'organised'. Yes, ESTJs are organised and we are planful. How I do it, I do not know … I just am organised. In grade school, I would always do my homework first and then work on my Girl Scout badges. (I earned a lot of badges!) However, I am not organised about everything because some things have a much lower priority, for example, the details of running a household. If it's a high priority to me, I'll organise it; if it's not, I won't.

For many people, part of being organised is following a standard operating procedure. That certainly is true for me, unless those procedures are inefficient, illogical, stupid and/or they simply do not work. I will follow decent procedures, and, in fact, I kind of like them. If no procedures exist, I make them. For example, the recommended method of validating type for research purposes is based on procedures I developed in the early 1980s. I do not like to reinvent the wheel and find redoing and reinventing things that already exist to be a (stupid) waste of time. Lists are great ways of keeping me on track and keeping track of what I need to do. There are very few days ever when I do not have a list, even when I'm on holiday.

ESTJs' dominant function is extraverted Thinking. Some people say we appear somewhat cool, calculating and detached. I prefer to look at it as objective, logical and focused; I enjoy making decisions. I like people to give me reasons for things and I have a hard time accepting an answer unless it is logical. I like being in situations where I can analyse and critique and make decisions. In fact, for me not to be able to critique is exceedingly difficult; I love to be picky – about the right things, of course – but there are times when I am concerned that I sound too critical and negative in the process. I have certain friends now with whom I have a pact that we critique everything. It's such fun to do in the privacy of our own homes or offices; we know better than to do that critiquing in public!

One thing I enjoy doing is writing and critiquing my own and others' writing. This led to the nickname of the 'Slasher' in one organisation for whom I worked; whenever they needed a piece of writing tightened up, they would bring it to me and I would do the job! That nickname eventually led me to a stalled editing job with the publisher of the MBTI® instrument. I recently finished a project working with my 96-year-old father, a food scientist, editing his scientific work on nutritional concepts. The critiquing part is fun, but the translating part is difficult – taking his scientific theories and translating them into laypersons' language. That requires my third function, Intuition, but more on that later.

For me, my Thinking is supreme. It's as if I have a 'decision tree' in my head – I can branch to the logical task side or I can branch to the relationships side. I always branch to that logical side; I can't help it. It's like those divining sticks held by someone searching for water in the desert. There's an irresistible pull when water is underneath the sand and there's an irresistible pull toward that logic.

I have learned that I must at some point pay attention to that people side, but to remember to do it is hard. I've named the necessary action as my 'circle the wagons' time. (I used to have a fascination with pioneer women settling the western part of the USA; they were in those wagon trains meeting each challenge head on and in practical ways. They would move their wagons into a circle to protect themselves from outside forces. It was through joining forces and forging relationships that they were able to get the task of protection done.) I try to make sure that by the end of the project, I've talked with each person personally to thank them for their contributions to the task, and in this way I've made sure my circle has included everyone and thus we're all protected.

My extraverted Thinking feels so easy, wonderful and multifaceted to me. I can put logical structure on things ... I can critique ... I can find flaws in advance ... I can see the pluses and minuses to anything ... I can develop procedures to get work done ... I see to the core of the matter ... I can eliminate the fluff ... I can be quickly decisive ... I can analyse thoroughly ... I can ... I can ... I can .... By the way, extraverted Thinking also appears as outward confidence and the majority of leaders throughout the world have extraverted Thinking as either their dominant or their auxiliary function. We certainly can do lots of things, but we have to be careful that we are doing the 'right' things in the 'right' ways as well.

My auxiliary function is my introverted Sensing. One of the ways I enjoy using that function is through reading, research and editing. I simply lose myself to the quiet of that introverted side and feel a real sense of peacefulness of purpose. I love to gather facts, whether that be the research portion of a paper or the details of the political climate in a company or the results of career inventories. I like to sit down, ponder the data, pull it together, reorder it for even greater logic, and look for connections. But I do not gather facts without a purpose – there has to be a practical and logical need for the data.

I like details and I find a certain satisfaction from having those details and facts organised. I like to be prepared. I seldom make errors of fact and

I have a good memory. I like to remember people and their types. However, in my 60s, I began to notice that my brain cells for some of that detail seem full to capacity. I can no longer remember this information readily. Even when I get those names from workshops I teach into my short-term memory, it's as if the hard drive gets wiped at the end of the session and those names are gone. I apologise in advance if you are one of those.

I am good at giving directions, and I like to give them. My S and T are working hand in hand then. There's a family story we tell about a trip to my mother-in-law's house and my INFP husband, John. Her home was about two miles from ours. John has a tendency to daydream, admiring the architecture of the homes (a value of his), and forget to turn soon enough to make the trip as efficiently as possible. We might even go an extra few blocks! When I pointed out the turn to him, I think my exact words were, 'Aren't you going to turn here!' He replied, 'You know Jean, if you continue to give me directions all the rest of our lives, you are never going to know if or when I get Alzheimer's disease.' At another point we had an interesting discussion on the definition of 'being lost'. Mine is 'not knowing how to get from point A to point B in the most direct, efficient way as possible' – see that ST coming into my thought process?! His is 'gaining no positive benefit from my current surroundings'. I have to admit that, at times, his definition comes in handy. Even though we are no longer married, I did learn a lot from our differences.

I also like to do Sensing things such as balancing our chequebook. None of my family members understands the satisfaction I get through looking at financial details and coming up with a bottom-line sum, even when that sum is negative. Doing this on a Friday night when, according to some, I should just be starting to enjoy the weekend is great timing. For me, it is when the details I am responsible for are organised that I can start to enjoy life.

My Sensing also helps me remember stories about people and anecdotes I can use in helping others understand psychological type. It helps me recall important information about people, and I use that as a way to connect with others as I ask about a family member or a trip they were talking about taking the last time we met. More recently, it helps me write eulogies for dear friends who have died; it is a gift I can give to their families and friends as I recall stories about them and their characters. That process also involves using my Intuition and Feeling.

Some of my Sensing delights come through travelling and noticing and experiencing new things. I love the details of a place and my memories of them. My first trip to England was in 1963; I still recall vividly the red tile roofs and the green grass I could see from the air flying into Heathrow. To make my trips to Oxford even more memorable, I set a goal to visit every one of the 35 colleges; I even set logical parameters to a visit – I had to see at least two quadrangles or the equivalent in each college. (Notice how I put Sensing into a logical framework.) Yes, that goal has been met. In North America, I've set a goal of working in every state of the USA and every province of Canada. (For those interested, I'm over three-quarters the way there!) Now that I'm near retirement, I'm substituting that goal with visiting as many UNESCO World Heritage sites as possible – they are sites of cultural and/or natural importance to humanity. I like trying out different things for the adventure involved – rock climbing, skydiving, hot air ballooning, race car driving, etc. I've done those once each and that was enough for me. I can even make an adventure out of standing in a long line (like when airport security changes), learning about the people around me and keeping up people's spirits as we wait. What is even more fun than the actual event is remembering the details of it and telling others. That skydiving episode likely was five minutes long, but I can go on for hours about it! My Sensing too seems like a good friend to me.

My tertiary function is my Intuition, and I find it both extravert and introvert depending on the circumstances. My understanding of my tertiary has grown much in the last three decades; I now see many more facets to it than I did when I was younger, but probably not as many as Intuitives do. I am not brilliant with intuitions, connections and seeing that big picture. I eventually get to the big picture through following my S and T. When I was younger, the essay portions of exams that asked me to conceptualise were always difficult. However, I studied long and hard and got enough facts together, including other people's theories, so I could at least throw in enough data and hope that they fit together enough to show a bit of intuition. I no longer take essay exams (thank goodness!), but I do write a lot and find I must make extra efforts to make sure the themes I want are there and the big picture is apparent. I now find it fun to look for the connections and theories in what I write.

I confess I used to define theories as big words strung together to explain the world in unrealistic ways. Obviously that meant that theories did not come naturally. Even now, when people ask me theoretically based questions I find myself glazing over, having to concentrate to pay attention and answering occasionally with an 'I don't know, but that's an interesting question.' However, I have found myself compelled (and even interested) to look more at theories recently because I believe theories are a good way to summarise my own and others' experiences; in this way they have a logical purpose. I have learned to search for theories in topics of interest. Two theories that are particularly helpful in my work are the Jung/Myers' theories of psychological type and the theories of Alfred Adler with his focus on the need for people to belong, cooperate and contribute to society. These are theories I can work with!!

Luckily for me, there are lots of theory and idea people running around the world, and many of them write and talk about them. I simply collect their ideas and adapt them. I love coming up with little twists on things other people have already thought of. I use my Intuition to change things to make them better. I also use it to be zany at times, to come up with playful turns of words, and to see the humour in life.

I have been associated for nearly two decades with a community leadership development programme for small towns in my state of Minnesota. Small towns won't survive without good leadership and this community leadership programme, fully funded by a charity (the Blandin Foundation), provides this. Most of the staff working in the programme are introverted Intuitives; the program is very theory based and we design curricula together based on theories of leadership, communication, power, conflict management, etc. That has forced me to see the value of the theories as a guideline to action (in fact, they even talk about the theory of action!).

As a Sensing psychologist, I used to feel terribly inferior amongst my Intuitive colleagues because I didn't see what they saw. I didn't trust my sense of what was going on to make connections with the themes in people's lives. But now I do. I suddenly gain insights on what is happening with people. Analogies and metaphors appear in my head and I see pictures that my clients find valuable. My ISFP client is describing two possible career choices: in my pictures, one lacks a core but has many trappings on the periphery, and one has a core that radiates warmth; I describe these pictures and my client knows instantly which career is for him (warmth!). I have figured out metaphors to explain each one of the eight dominant functions and often use them in training to help others understand them, e.g., 'tornado' for ET and 'filing cabinet' for IS. But I always attach words to those metaphors and explain them in detail, and not just let them stand on their own. Metaphors still need translation, and one of the things that drives me crazy about Intuitives is that they often don't translate their metaphors. I also am still learning to look beneath the surface – what a person says isn't always what's the important message. I would rather accept things at face value, but I know that I shouldn't.

My inferior function is my introverted Feeling function, and that is my most difficult function. Some people describe ESTJs as focusing solely on the logic and forgetting the value of emotions and feelings. How wrong they are! We care, we have emotions and feelings – but remember, we also introvert them. They are different than the other aspects of our lives that we do control more firmly.

[Note: I do not mean to equate Feeling with emotions, but I believe Feeling types pay more attention to their emotions and trust them more than Thinking types. Their emotions are guides to their values and what will create harmony and hence their best decisions. Thinking types often keep their emotions at arm's length and don't let them guide their decisions quite as much. We need to learn what they mean, but for us they have been more unreliable.]

Luckily, I am clear on my basic values; I was raised by an INFP mother who instilled strong human welfare values early on and to whom I am forever grateful. My upbringing was very affirming of me. My entire family has IN preferences. I think my parents somehow sensed I was different from them and always encouraged my extraverted development, perhaps because they thought it was something they had struggled with in growing up. They passed on to me a great deal of N and F. My father, as an immigrant to the United States, got a chance because of American values. If he had remained in Europe, he would have been an unskilled labourer and likely killed in the Second World War; in the United States, he became a university professor. Yes, N and F, giving people chances, recognising uniqueness and making a difference in people's lives was/is important. But I act upon those in an ST manner.

I chose a career as a psychologist partly out of my human welfare value system. When I applied for graduate school, I applied for a counselling and student personnel programme. I had planned to be a college administrator, not a counsellor or therapist. My graduate programme, however, was not what it appeared to be and actually was counselling training. For many years, I felt lumps in my stomach when listening to people explain their problems to me. At those times, I could not trust my own F enough to feel good about helping others. It was scary. Yet that experience was also incredibly broadening, but one I did not fully understand until I learned about psychological type several years later. Jobs in university administration were not available when I completed my degree and I moved my career to management consulting, career counselling and training. In retrospect, these too have been wonderful ways to use my ST.

About 15 years ago, I participated in a type and imagery session. I have never felt comfortable with visualisation techniques and was bothered by this for only one reason. What if I should get cancer and need to use visualisations and imagery in treatment ... what would I do? (Such is the mind of a practical ESTJ!) In this session and subsequent ones I was able to visualise all four of my functions and found all had much meaning for me. My visualisation of my fourth function was that of a glacier melting. Yes, slowly my Feeling was being exposed no matter what I did! (I just wish that global warming weren't actually speeding the real glaciers melting!)

Even though I have a clear sense of values, I still can have trouble with the F side in consistently appreciating my own and others' value and remembering what's really important in life. Having been married and a parent has been helpful here, and my children continually remind me of what is most important even though they are launched and in the world. I'm particularly proud that they are both global citizens, with my daughter living in Australia and my son in Hong Kong.

I don't always remember to compliment people when I should and let them know how appreciated they are, but I'm working on that. I make it a regular practice to send out thank you notes and comment on wonderful things my friends and colleagues have done. I am learning to value my friends more and to spend as much time with them as possible; having lost so many to cancer, this is especially important to me. Although I work in my own business, I am associated with two dynamic groups of colleagues, including those who work with psychological type. The other group are my colleagues in the Blandin community leadership programme. I coordinate and supervise a staff of people in that community leadership programme and one of the things I feel proudest of is having made it possible for them to forge close friendships with one another. Being a professional in a small town can be lonely, and these folks have been so supportive of one another. Please let the record show here how appreciative I am of these colleagues. I also have good friends from as far back as age 12 with whom I have regular reunions (we are scattered throughout the USA), college friends, book club friends, etc. and make efforts to keep connected with them.

My F can sneak up on me in a variety of situations. I may get goose bumps describing a particularly meaningful interaction with a client, especially when I give them another way to understand a situation and some tools to deal with it. I feel tears of pride when one of my children does something special. I can feel it in the pit of my stomach when a group is acting in an inappropriate way. I used to attempt to either ignore those signs or logically analyse them. Now I try to let those emotions and feelings be clues to my F and acknowledge their existence. I may say something out loud to acknowledge those feelings. Later I start to logically analyse them to bring meaning and have them make sense. But their origins are very different than what I'm used to. And because they come from my inferior function I have less control over them and less understanding of them.

Learning to live with the deaths of people close to me has also led to some F development. When my grandmother suffered a stroke and was unable to communicate, I instinctively took her hand and started telling her all my happy memories of her; she started to cry and I did too. I got to tell her goodbye in a very meaningful way. I have had so many good friends live and die with cancer. Holding hands with them, working hand lotion into their skin, talking with them about life, telling them that I care about them, hugging them good-bye ... well, words can't describe that meaning to me. One friend, Susan Brock, asked me to be part of a group, a healing circle, supporting her as she lived with cancer. We developed a spiritual ritual and met for several years; she far outlived her life 'expectancy' and with a much greater quality of life. Seeing her drag into a meeting with no energy and bounce out with a renewed sense of life ... it was/is a priceless experience. Since then I have organised and participated in several other healing circles and occasionally teach classes on a volunteer basis on how to 'do' them. I also have taught classes to people in health crises on how to manage stress through utilising psychological type principles. When someone tells me a family member or friend has died, I now more easily can express sympathy and ask them to tell me a memory; I've heard many special stories as a result.

I have had to deal with other crises in my life – things that have changed my direction. A major one was the end of my marriage for reasons that were truly out of my control. It was the relationships I had forged through the years that helped me through those crises and transitions, not my logical thinking. Friends flew in from out of town to help me move and set up a new household; others checked in regularly. The events are still difficult to fully understand and explain, but perhaps next time you'll hear of those. In spite of, or perhaps because of, those changes, I've found myself making new friendships and enjoying life even more now.

One question I was asked after my original panel presentation is, 'How did it feel to reveal so much of myself?' Off the top of my head I said, 'Fine, after all, I have been through counsellor training where that was expected and therefore done.' But upon reflection, I realised that getting to F still brought up different uncomfortable feelings, lumps in my throat or whatever, when I chose to pay attention. I did not/could not reveal all of those inner feelings to the audience nor even to myself. I'm still working on my Feeling function, and I can get emotional in front of a group as I describe my experience of it, but I don't mind showing those emotions now. The actual work seems at times to be just letting it come and recognising it and accepting it. It is still amorphous, but that feels just fine now! Even dominant introverted Feeling types have trouble describing their function in words. I'll accept that it exists and is wonderful too.

Now I've come full circle, taking you through my type development that really follows my type dynamics. Please remember a key characteristic of ESTJs: we set a goal and go after it. My goal was to briefly explain ESTJs through one ESTJ's path of development. I hope I have. And I invite you to explore your own path as well. Thank you to Rowan Bayne for providing me with this opportunity to revisit my own development; this is my fourth opportunity to do so. Perhaps in another decade or so, I'll be lucky enough to be asked to edit this once again and see what I have learned and/or accepted.

DEVELOPING MY PREFERENCES AND NON-PREFERENCES, BY AN INFPC

This case study is my view of my own development (in terms of preferences and non-preferences). Five themes summarise my life so far:

- love of words;
- love of sport;
- finding some things (activities, areas of study) easy and fun, others not at all appealing *and* not doing them (which sounds lucky and uncomfortably arrogant);
- searching for romantic love;
- needing and finding lots of time alone.

Each of these themes reflects my preferences for I, N, F ,P and C and my non-preferences for E, S, T, J and W.

Love of words

I have written two short stories and two very short poems. I wrote them when I was a child and decided then that these forms of writing, let alone novels etc., are not for me and seem very unlikely to become so.

When I was about eight, I would often go to the public library, take a book (a novel) out, read it there and return it. I also remember getting piles of books (and socks and handkerchiefs) every Christmas from early in my life – novels by Enid Blyton, particularly the *Far Away Tree* series, and later Arthur Ransome, and then as a teenager the classics and lots of science fiction.

As an adult I read, and in retirement will reread, literary, psychological novelists like John Updike, Carol Shields, Marge Piercy, Margaret Atwood, Fay Weldon and Iris Murdoch, as well as textbooks on counselling and personality. Equally good clues for N and F are what I rarely read – almost every other genre – and why I read: for beauty of expression and insights into people, for example the extracts from Carol Shields in Chapter 1. Two other examples that come to mind are 'We contain chords that others must strike' (from one of John Updike's *Rabbit* books) and 'As he relaxed, I suffocated' (a relationship shortly after marriage, economically and eloquently summarised by the leading character in Julie Myerson's first novel, *Sleepwalking*).

Love of sport

As a male who prefers F, my time at school was made easier by being good at football and sprinting. I also played the clown quite successfully, but this was partly because I was often bored by the lessons.

Appealing and repelling activities

The only subject I really enjoyed at school was English literature and I still have narrow (or specialised) interests. My most treasured confirmation of this quality is from a school report when I was 14: my physics teacher wrote two words, presumably in despair and exasperation, perhaps anger, 'Thoroughly idle'. I can sympathise now but didn't at the time. This school subject and my lack of effort in something I had no interest in are clues for F and P although I know an INFP with a First in physics. Most things do not interest me, including cars and computers. At school I was often in trouble but only when I was bored and for minor offences.

In writing, I love rewriting and editing and being a 'translator' of theories and research to help practitioners, as I hope is apparent in this book! At school, writing a précis was much more fun than making up a story.

Looking for romantic love

Too personal to write about here, but I would structure my life story mainly around relationships.

Time alone

I had bronchitis often as a child, which meant many happy hours reading in bed, but I tried living alone, for a year in my early fifties, and didn't like it. I was at boarding school from about 16 to 18 years old, sleeping in a dormitory, and found it restorative and essential to make time to be by myself – more so than any of my peers. I felt 'jangly' if I didn't, a clue for I, though this difference between I and E in amount of time needed alone is a matter of degree. (Most Es need some time alone, just as most Is need some contact with other people.)

Other preferences and non-preferences

P is evident through my energetic and unstressed reaction to deadlines (a clue discussed in Chapter 2), lack of plans and treatment of lists (discussed early in Chapter 2). I find the skills of my non-preference for T very hard even after all these years of studying, teaching and research. Carol Shields' phrase 'at the frontier' (discussed in Chapter 1) fits so well. I *have* developed my T and it's occasionally very sharp – it feels like a laser then – but it's not predictable when this will happen and it doesn't last long. I remember enjoying creating a complex flow chart (a pure T activity), but I've only created one more in the 20 years since. Also, although I can be steely, I'm most myself when being gentle and encouraging, and quiet!

The preference for C or W isn't included by Jean in her ESTJ description because it's not part of standard psychological type theory. I've only recently come to appreciate CW as a preference and, applying it to myself, clues for C are a calm approach to most problems and setbacks (though *not* when computers or other machines go wrong or when other people try to control me), a quick recovery from relationship problems and break-ups, and being generally optimistic and trusting – naively so in the view of someone I know well who prefers W.

Overall I see myself, in the preference domain of personality, as an INFPC with good development (though scope for more) of those five preferences; some good E skills, helped by F, especially meeting people when we both have roles, but awkward and uncomfortable, so far, in unstructured situations; some development of aspects of S, though I'm often struck, when I'm with someone who prefers S, by how pale and undeveloped my S is; and some development of T, J and W, but again patchy.

Chapter 8

Increasing Self-awareness 3: Discovering Life Stories

This chapter discusses:

- the place of integrative life stories or life narratives in applied personality theory;
- how and when to suggest to a client using a technique for exploring life stories;
- some approaches to exploring life stories, including scripts, the life story interview, self-defining memories and archetypes;
- analysing and reconstructing life stories.

McAdams' model of personality suggests that each of three domains adds separately to our understanding of personality. Each domain is a legitimate aspect of personality in itself. Integrative life stories is his third domain, and is about how we make sense of the way our personality has expressed itself and unfolded over our lifetime; how we integrate our past, present and future selves. Thus we integrate new events, hopes and fears and develop new insights and understandings as we, perhaps slowly, find our place in the world.

Researchers into life stories argue that the tendency to see and create such stories (as with patterns generally) is a human characteristic. They see us in adulthood as working on our life stories often, especially after major transitions and experiences. At such times, we may change or develop our life story. There are times of rapid and dramatic change in our stories and times of stability and consolidation. Life stories are both continuous and changing (McAdams, 2009).

Having a 'good' life story is related to mental health (Lilgendahl & McAdams, 2011; Adler, 2012). The extensive research on the related topic of expressive writing about troubling experiences and emotions (e.g., Pennebaker et al., 1990; Lyubomirsky et al., 2006; Pennebaker, 2012) demonstrates clearly the value of expression and reflection for physical health, too, and suggests that the writing *causes* the good health rather than being caused by it. It is plausible that constructing a coherent and positive life story is similarly beneficial. One of Pennebaker's findings is that use of words indicating causes and insights (i.e., an analysis stage following reflection) is particularly effective, a point developed in the section on analysing and reconstructing life stories.

McAdams' approach to life stories emphasises the roles of integration and coherence. While life stories are dynamic and evolving, the good stories express a meaningful identity. For him (e.g., McAdams, 2009), a good life story also shows considerable openness to change and to a variety of options for the future. However, he may here be showing a bias towards preferences for N and P: according to preference theory, people who prefer S and J are healthy and happy with detailed plans and with carrying them out.

Perhaps, though, we vary much more than integrative life stories, let alone preferences and motives, propose: reality may not be so tidy. This constructivist view is that personality, in the stable, coherent sense, doesn't exist. Rather, we make it up to help us cope. More radically, constructivism assumes that there is no objective reality (McLeod, 2009). The realist view is directly opposed to constructivism. It assumes that personality in the sense of preferences, motives and life stories does exist and that questions about it are sensible and useful; that there is an inner essence which can be discovered, actualised, clarified or denied. I'll consider both views in the section on analysing and reconstructing life stories.

HOW AND WHEN TO SUGGEST EXPLORING LIFE STORIES

Some clients find it helpful to work on their life stories (Singer, 2005). Even at a simple level of exploration, they can discover something surprising and useful and make more sense of their life and of themselves. Other clients want more depth. However, sometimes the best option is not to explore the life story – some events are so traumatic that clients choose not to share them or to protect themselves from even thinking about them, at least in the short term. That is the client's right, of course – the principle of client autonomy applies, even though it may be unhealthy to deny or minimise the impact of the experiences for long.

What if a client wants to explore aspects of their life story which you do not feel competent to deal with? Or to explore their life story at all when you think it inappropriate for them or for you? Norcross and Wampold (2011b) noted that they are often asked in presentations and workshops what they would do if they were unable or unwilling to adapt their approach to a client in ways supported by the research on matching. They briefly discussed four possibilities: (1) to address the matter 'forthrightly'; (2) to discuss treatment options and choosing between them with their client; (3) to choose clients who fit their approach; and (4) 'judicious referral'. These aspects of matching (and not matching) of counsellor and client are discussed in Chapter 4.

The next section reviews methods of accessing and exploring life stories. Researchers in the area find that generally we need help to do this (e.g., Raggatt, 2006).

SOME METHODS FOR EXPLORING LIFE STORIES

A simple approach to writing a life story is to just write (say) about 1000 words on yourself. This can be in any form you or your client choose, and it may be helpful to write it in the third person and from the perspective of someone who knows you well.

Coherent life stories have structures and there are numerous possibilities for these in life stories. You may like to pause at this point and reflect on possible structures for your own life story.

The life-line exercise familiar to many counsellors through their training offers a structure of time. Some other possibilities are places you've lived, life events you see as pivotal and your close relationships, as in William Boyd's novel *Any Human Heart*, which is structured in terms of the eight women the narrator had loved or who had dominated a period of his life.

Scripts

Another possibility focuses more on early childhood. This is the idea in transactional analysis of scripts (Steiner, 1974; Berne, 1975) – that we learn a set of beliefs early in childhood about how the rest of our life is going to be. For example, someone who cares for an ill parent and has little time for other activities may see this as the central meaning of their life and seek out caring roles as an adult in a compulsive, automatic way. Our script thus includes values, desires, beliefs and goals and it underlies behaviour.

The idea of scripts is fundamentally related to that of a real self, with scripts being obstacles to self-actualisation. In Berne's view, we are each ruled by our script and dutifully play the roles it prescribes. A script is learnt from repeated 'messages' from powerful sources, most obviously parents and guardians but also social class and culture. The messages can be from behaviour – for example, a parent who is very driven by work demonstrating that life is serious – or from direct comments made many times such as 'You're so clumsy' and 'You're such a pretty little girl'. Some messages are positive and liberating – for example, 'It's ok to express feelings' – while others create scripts, which are restricting by definition.

Scripts can be uncovered through script analysis. One approach is to use questions such as, 'What do your parents say when they criticise you?', 'What could you do to make them happy?', 'What words do you fear might appear in your epitaph?' (the last question is moving into existential concerns but as a way of uncovering past influences), 'What were you told about your grandparents?', 'How old do you expect to be when you die?' (Steiner, 1974, wrote that Berne's script told him that he'd die at 60, that Berne knew this, and that he died at 60 anyway).

One or two of these questions may be enough to uncover significant aspects of a script and life story, though not necessarily at once: memories may come up in the next days and weeks, and your script gradually appears. It's not a magical or mystical process and the values and beliefs etc. can be examined and replaced, and a new set of decisions made about your life.

The life story interview

McAdams developed a more elaborate system for exploring life stories: a Life Story Interview in which the interviewee is asked first to think about their life as if it were a book with chapters, and then to identify each chapter and outline its contents, like a plot summary. Next, she or he is asked to describe eight key scenes from their story, each depicting one of the following events: a high point, a low point, a turning point, earliest memory, important childhood episode, important adolescent episode, important adult episode and one other important episode.

There are five further stages in the life story interview, which seems likely to be too many for most counsellors and clients. Briefly, these stages are describing the biggest challenge faced by the participant and how they met it; the character with the most positive effect on their life and the one with the most negative effect; an account of where the story is going, for example main goals, dreams and fears; questions on values, and religious and political beliefs; and finally, identifying a single integrative theme.

At each stage the interviewer can vary in how probing they are and in their use of theory, for example Piaget or Erikson (Singer, 2005; McAdams, 2009), to guide their questions. Similarly, some clients and counsellors may include a client's parents and family background. Again, this emphasis may be too elaborate or time consuming, and the options chosen will be influenced by your client's problems and goals and perhaps by your intuitions. In my view, the first stage, the second, or both, of the life story interview work well and are often sufficient.

Self-defining memories

An intermediate approach which includes an integrative element is to ask about 'self-defining memories' (Singer, 2005: 88–90). The instructions, paraphrased here, ask the client to imagine that they've just met someone they like very much and that they go for a walk. They and the other person want to know each other quickly and deeply and they both describe memories to show the kind of person they are. In counselling, you ask your client, probably between sessions, to recall ten memories each with the following characteristics:

1. You are at least a year old.
2. You remember it very clearly and it feels important now.
3. It's about an enduring issue that explains part of who you are as an individual.
4. You think about it quite often.

Archetypes

Archetypes are a possible short cut to identifying integrative themes in a life story. An archetype can be defined as 'an internal mental model of a typical generic story character to which an observer might resonate emotionally' (Faber & Mayer, 2009: 397). While this definition is accurate and useful, it does not capture the daring and power of Jung's concept and it deliberately excludes the central mystical aspect of archetypes: the idea that when a person or event arouses an archetype in you it then takes over and has you in its grip.

Jung proposed that these patterns of energy or roles lie waiting in the depths of our personalities, in what he called the 'collective unconscious', which contains ancestral memories of the shared experiences and wisdom of all generations of humankind. He saw them as similar to instincts in other animals – genetically programmed ways of behaving which are activated by certain recurring situations such as fighting or becoming a mother.

Jung came to these ideas through his reading of philosophical, religious and mystical texts in a wide range of cultures. Some interpreters of Jung see them as real, like a house or a bus. Jung himself wrote that archetypes, which are the main elements of the collective unconscious, 'are not mere objects of the mind but are also autonomous factors' (1969: 469).

The idea of a collective unconscious may make some sense from an evolutionary perspective. Our brains have evolved in the face of common threats and tasks and the archetypes can be generally understood as universal themes of human experience over time and cultures which are prominent in art, literature, dreams, visions, myths, fairy tales and films. People create their identities in part by identifying with some of these stories in their families and cultures, but can change. For example, certain behaviours and feelings may be associated with gender. Thus, a young man taught not to cry as a child sees a man he admires in tears or meets someone who takes a different view – 'That's what our fathers' generation do. When I'm upset, I cry' – which he then integrates into his own identity.

Examples of archetypes are Hero, Earth Mother, Trickster and Sage (Table 8.1). Nehrer (1996), in an incisive critique, sees them as a 'handy framework' for the easy understanding of behaviour – though, as he also says, the important question is 'What is valid?', not 'What is easy?' However, archetypes may have some value as narratives, scripts or stories. If the idea of archetypes is valid, then awareness of our particular archetype or archetypes at this point in our lives gives us more choice and the possibility of harnessing its power rather than being controlled by it. Some archetypes fit us, some we outgrow, some we grow into.

Faber and Mayer (2009) proposed a new theory of archetypes and tested their reasoning that 'if archetypes exist ... these affective schemas or mental models can be identified in the popular music, movies, television, literature and classic art of today' (2009: 310). They did find such relationships, and interpreted them as 'surprising new evidence for the possible existence of dominant archetypal themes in our lives' (p. 320). For example, 'Carers' tend to enjoy romantic movies and fashion books and 'Strivers' tend to enjoy action movies, sports TV and books about

Table 8.1 Examples of archetypes and associated qualities

Archetype	Qualities
The Warrior	Vigour and bravery
The Lover	Striving for intimacy
The Innocent	Trusting and optimistic
The Sage	Seeking wisdom
The Earth Mother	Devoted to others and putting them first

spies. The authors speculate that archetypal themes will also predict social behaviour, complementing and adding to predictions from personality traits and social roles. Further, such themes may be useful in designing more effective advertising and health messages as well as in therapy.

Faber and Mayer (2009) list the music tracks they used as part of their measure of archetypes. You may like to think of your favourite tracks and what they may say about your identity. Examples from Faber and Mayer's research are 'Paranoid Android' (by Radiohead) representing the archetypal theme of The Sage, 'Angel of Death' (by Slayer) representing The Shadow, and 'It's Oh So Quiet' (by Bjork) representing The Innocent.

Pearson and Marr (2007) have developed a questionnaire, which is commercially available (at www.capt.org), called the Pearson–Marr Archetype Indicator. They focus on 12 common archetypes: the Innocent, Orphan, Warrior, Care-giver, Seeker, Lover, Creator, Destroyer, Ruler, Magician, Sage and Jester. All have both positive and negative aspects: for example, the Innocent is described as trusting others, but sometimes too much, and relying on others, again perhaps too much.

Pearson and Marr stress that answers to the questionnaire are not a substitute for the person's own judgement. Rather, they are a mirror 'to help you have a conversation with yourself and others about the stories that influence your life and that create or inhibit the satisfaction you get from life' (2007: 28). They also include ideas about associated hidden motives and life scripts and ways of changing them.

ANALYSING AND RECONSTRUCTING LIFE STORIES

Of the many ways to analyse a life story (Singer, 2005; McAdams, 2009), three general approaches are the most relevant to counselling: first, the *constructivist*, which accepts 'a swirl of fleeting stories and postures' (McAdams, 2006: 477) and, as touched on earlier, neglects (or rejects) a unified and stable self; second, the *psychodynamic*, in which there are layers of meanings and the most insightful meanings are hidden; third, the *humanistic*, which assumes that we live our stories relatively consciously but that we may benefit from adding more depth and detail and from reflecting on and possibly reinterpreting their meaning.

Any or all of these general approaches may be used with a particular client, the key question being: 'What does this aspect say about who you are and who you might be?' To answer this question, counsellor and client look for insights, beliefs and alternative interpretations. They edit and create. For example, a client's main theme might be that they have been faced with many obstacles but have resiliently overcome them, and they might choose to continue in their life with this theme, or refine it or reject it. Singer (2005) gives the example of a client whose theme was to 'keep my family happy', and again the client might choose to maintain this identity or to change it. Thus a life story's integrative theme can be treated in the same way as an irrational belief is treated in CBT.

John McLeod (2009) outlined several ideas for working with narratives in a constructivist way, though they seem useful generally as well. Among them are adopting a '*not knowing* stance' (2009: 236, italics in original), by which he means treating the client as the expert on their story and on how to change it, and 'externalising the problem'. Externalising the problem means separating the story from the client – there is more to them than their problem or their dominant story, and when the client recognises this it opens up the possibility of reinterpreting their story.

Such a recognition is achieved first by naming the problem in the client's words as specifically as possible. Clients' stories are often 'thin' in narrative therapy terms: that is, connecting a small number of events, lacking depth and detail, and being interpreted in ways that are too simple and negative. For example, 'I've been sacked from my last three jobs, I'm a failure at work and I've given up trying to find a job.' One approach is to treat the story as if it's a basis for a film or a novel by naming central and minor characters, and identifying the plot, subplots and themes. The story can then, if the process is working, be 're-authored'. For example, a story about failure might become a story about survival and inner resources.

The client may also usefully explore how their story and interpretation (the narrative) has stayed unchallenged and powerful, and how it influences them, with both of you looking out for times when the narrative and resulting problems were *not* strong and did not dominate them. These moments are called 'sparkling moments' in narrative therapy, and are the basis of reinterpreting the story. Externalising can take place through questioning or, more collaboratively, through conversation, poetry, music. I see the counsellor as an editor here, but one who generally raises rather than suggests answers (tempting though that may be).

The process of exploring (and analysing) life stories is likely to be emotional. Therefore it is important, as it is in counselling generally, to bear in mind a principle stated well by Irvin Yalom (2001): that 'effective therapy consists of an alternating sequence: *evocation and experiencing* of affect followed by *analysis and integration* of affect' (2001: 71, italics in original). Yalom also commented on a key practical aspect of this principle: 'How long one waits until one initiates an analysis of the affective event is a function of clinical experience' (p. 71), which is not so helpful! Kennedy-Moore and Watson (1999) are more specific when they suggest that a client who is 'flooding' – caught up in an emotion for several minutes or longer – should be offered distraction techniques like counting backwards in sevens from 300, or breathing slowly and deeply, to help them regain enough composure to reflect and analyse.

James Pennebaker (2012) has a related view, based on his and others' research on writing about traumatic events, which was discussed briefly in the introductory section of this chapter. He sees telling the same traumatic stories again and again as unhelpful or worse, because it tends to lead to depression. He recommends a variety of techniques: alternative interpretations (reframing), writing in the third person, using the words 'I' and 'me' more often, writing from the point of view of one or more of the other people in the story (switching between one's own perspective, their perspective and back again), and looking for what is good in the story while not underemphasising the bad aspects.

CONCLUDING COMMENT

The last few years have been an especially productive and exciting time for personality and counselling researchers, and what I've tried to do is bring together some of the best ideas and evidence in each area in a way that counsellors will find helpful. The artistic side of being a counsellor, like the individuality of each personality, will always be there, but good theory and research complement and enhance the artistry, as I hope you've found (or will find) in this book.

Further Resources

BOOKS AND ARTICLES

My top five recommendations for publications on personality and counselling are as follows:

Aron, E. N. (2010) *Psychotherapy and the Highly Sensitive Person. Improving Outcomes for That Minority of People Who Are the Majority of Clients*. London: Routledge.
Note the subtitle. This is an in-depth review which in my view will become a classic. The author is a researcher and psychotherapist and herself a Highly Sensitive Person.

Miller, T. (1991) 'The psychotherapeutic utility of the five-factor model of personality: a clinician's experience', *Journal of Personality Assessment* 57: 415–33.
Outstandingly clear, thoughtful and stimulating article by a very experienced therapist, though I've argued in this book that he is sometimes wrong, especially about people who prefer P. I recommend his professional website highly too.

Provost, J. A. (1993) *Applications of the Myers-Briggs Type Indicator in Counseling: A Casebook*, 2nd edn. Gainesville, FL: CAPT.
Brief and engaging case studies of just two to three pages each of the author's counselling with clients of each of the 16 MBTI types and two clients who are unclear about one of their preferences.

Tieger, P. D. and Barron-Tieger, B. (2007) *Do What You Are: Discover the Perfect Career for You through the Secrets of Personality Type*, 4th edn. London: Little, Brown.

Tieger, P. D. and Barron-Tieger, B. (2000) *Just Your Type: The Relationship You've Always Wanted Using the Secrets of Personality Type*. London: Little, Brown.
Don't be misled by the 'pop psychology' titles and subtitles. These books are evidence-based, unpretentious, lucid and very systematic and practical.

OTHER RESOURCES

1. The Internet

One of the best of the hundreds of MBTI sites is: **www.personalitytype.com**
This has brief profiles of each type, with sections on observing, loving and parenting each type, communicating and career choices.

Two others, each with a links section for easy transfer to other MBTI sites, are:
www.typetalk.com which is Otto Kroeger's site
www.teamtechnology.co.uk

2. Membership organisations

www.bapt.org.uk British Association for Psychological Type
www.aptinternational.org Association for Psychological Type

3. Research

- CAPT (Center for Applications of Psychological Type):
  www.capt.org
  Free online bibliography (10,000+ items) of research on psychological type and related topics. Select 'Research' and then 'Bibliographic Search'. Publishes and supplies MBTI books and the *Journal of Psychological Type*, and runs MBTI training in the USA.

4. Training in the UK

You need to be officially qualified to use the MBTI itself, either as a chartered psychologist or (more ethically) through specific training. OPP is the licensing body for Europe:
Telephone: 01865 404500
Website: www.opp.eu.com

References

Adler, J. M. (2012) Living into the story: agency and coherence in a longitudinal study of narrative identity development and mental health over the course of psychotherapy. *Journal of Personality and Social Psychology* 102: 367–89.

Allen, J. & Brock, S. A. (2000) *Health Care Communication and Personality Type*. London: Routledge.

Andrews, P. W. & Thomson, J. A. (2009) The bright side of being blue: depression as an adaptation for analyzing complex problems. *Psychological Review* 116: 620–54.

Aron, E. (1996) *The Highly Sensitive Person*. New York: Birch Lane Press.

Aron, E. (2010) *Psychotherapy and the Highly Sensitive Person: Improving Outcomes for That Minority of People Who Are the Majority of Clients*. London: Routledge.

Barger, N. & Kirby, L. (1993) The interaction of cultural values and type development: INTP women across cultures. *Bulletin of Psychological Type* 16: 14–16.

Barnes, S. (2011) *The Times*, 14 October 2011, p. 25.

Bayne, R. (2004) *Psychological Types at Work. An MBTI Perspective*. London: Thomson.

Bayne, R. (2005) *Ideas and Evidence. Critical Reflections on MBTI Theory and Practice*. Gainesville, FL: Center for Applications of Psychological Type.

Bayne, R. & Jinks, G. (2010) *How to Survive Counsellor Training: An A–Z Guide*. Basingstoke: Palgrave Macmillan.

Bayne, R., Jinks, G., Collard, P. & Horton, I. (2008) *The Counsellor's Handbook. A Practical A–Z Guide to Integrative Counselling and Psychotherapy*, 3rd edn. Cheltenham: Nelson Thornes.

Beer, A. & Brooks, C. (2011) Information quality in personality judgement: the value of personal disclosure. *Journal of Research in Personality* 45: 175–85.

Berens, L. V. (2000) *Understanding Yourself and Others: An Introduction to Temperament*. Huntington Beach, CA: Telos Publications.

Berens, L. V. & Nardi, D. (1999) *The Sixteen Personality Types: Descriptions for Self-Discovery*. Huntingdon Beach, CA: Telos Publications.

Berne, E. (1975) *What Do You Say After You Say Hello? The Psychology of Human Destiny*. New York: Grove Press.

Biddle, S. J. H. (2010) Physical activity. In D. French, K. Vedhara, A. A. Kaptein & J. Weinman (eds), *Health Psychology*, 2nd edn. Oxford: BPS Blackwell.

Bonanno, G. A. (2011) *The Other Side of Sadness: What the New Science of Bereavement Tells Us About Life After Loss*. London: Basic Books.

Brock, S. A. (1994) *Using Type in Selling*. Palo Alto, CA: CPP.
Brue, S. (2008) *The 8 Colors of Fitness*. Delroy Beach, FL: Oakledge Press.
Buckingham, M. & Clifton, D. O. (2001) *Now, Discover Your Strengths*. London: Simon and Schuster.
Bugental, J. F. T. & Bugental, E. K. (1980) The far side of despair. *Journal of Humanistic Psychology* 20: 49–68.
Carr, S. (1997) *Type Clarification: Finding the Fit*. Oxford: OPP.
Caspi, A., Roberts, B. W. & Shiner, R. L. (2005) Personality development: stability and change. *Annual Review of Psychology* 56: 453–84.
Cheek, J. M. & Buss, A. H. (1981) Shyness and sociability. *Journal of Personality and Social Psychology* 41: 330–9.
Chester, R. G. (2006) Asperger's syndrome and psychological type. *Journal of Psychological Type* 12: 114–37.
Cheston, R. & Bender, M. (2003) *Understanding Dementia*. London: Jessica Kingsley.
Churchill, S. (2011) *The Troubled Mind. A Handbook of Therapeutic Approaches to Psychological Distress*. Basingstoke: Palgrave Macmillan.
Churchill, S. & Bayne, R. (1998) Psychological type and different concepts of empathy in experienced counsellors. *Counselling Psychology Quarterly* 11: 379–90.
Cooper, M. (2008) *Essential Research Findings in Counselling and Psychotherapy*. London: Sage.
Corey, G. (2005) *Theory and Practice of Counselling and Psychotherapy*, 7th edn. London: Thomson.
Dahlstrom W. G. (1995) Pigeons, people and pigeon-holes. *Journal of Personality Assessment* 64: 2–20.
Darker, C. D., French, D. P., Eves, F. F. & Sniehotta, F. F. (2010) An intervention to promote walking amongst the general population based on an extended Theory of Planned Behaviour. *Psychology and Health* 25: 71–88.
Dean, G. (1986–7) Does astrology need to be true? *The Skeptical Inquirer* 11: 166–83, 257–73.
DiTiberio, J. K. & Hammer, A. L. (1993) *Introduction to Type in College*. Palo Alto, CA: Consulting Psychologists Press.
Dickson, A. (1987) *A Woman in Your Own Right*. London: Quartet.
Dodd, N. & Bayne, R. (2006) Psychological type and choice of counselling model by experienced counsellors. *Journal of Psychological Type* 11: 98–113.
Donnellan, M. B., Conger, R. D. & Bryant, C. M. (2004) The Big Five and enduring marriages. *Journal of Research in Personality* 38: 481–504.
Dosani, S. (2012) Working with adults with ADHD. *Therapy Today* (June): 22–5.
Dryden, W. (1991) *A Dialogue with Arnold Lazarus. It Depends*. Milton Keynes: Open University Press.
Dryden, W. (1998) *Are You Sitting Uncomfortably? Windy Dryden Live and Uncut*. Ross-on-Wye: PCCS Books.
Dryden, W. (2011) *Counselling in a Nutshell*, 2nd edn. London: Sage.
Duncan, B. L., Miller, S. D., Wampold, B. E. & Hubble, M. A. (eds) (2010) *The Heart and Soul of Change. Delivering What Works in Therapy*, 2nd edn. Washington, DC: APA.

Dunn, S. (2006) The MBTI instrument – a psychotherapeutic template for 'normal'? *Type Face* 17: 28–9.

Egan, G. (2010) *The Skilled Helper*, 9th edn. Monterey, CA: Brooks/Cole [preface].

Elliman, L. (2011) Asperger's syndrome – difference or disorder. *The Psychologist* 24: 114–17.

Emmons, R. A. (1986) Personal strivings: an approach to personality and subjective well-being. *Journal of Personality and Social Psychology* 51: 1058–68.

Emmons, R. A. & King, L. A. (1988) Conflict among personal strivings: immediate and long-term implications for psychological and physical well-being. *Journal of Personality and Social Psychology* 54: 1040–8.

Ericsson, K. A., Krampe, R. T. & Tesch-Roemer, C. (1993) The role of deliberate practice in the acquisition of expert performance. *Psychological Review* 100: 363–406.

Faber, M. A & Mayer, J. D. (2009) Resonance to archetypes in media: there's some accounting for taste. *Journal of Research in Personality* 43: 307–22.

Fleeson, W. & Gallagher, P. (2009) The implications of Big Five standing for the distribution of trait manifestation in behavior: fifteen experience-sampling studies and a meta-analysis. *Journal of Personality and Social Psychology* 97(6): 1097–114.

Fransella, F. & Dalton, P. (2000) *Personal Construct Counselling in Action*, 2nd edn. London: Sage.

French, D., Vedhara, K., Kaptein, A. A. & Weinman, J. (eds) (2010) *Health Psychology*, 2nd edn. Oxford: BPS Blackwell.

Funder, D. C. (2010) *The Personality Puzzle*, 5th edn. London: W. W. Norton.

Furnham, A. (1996) The big five versus the big four: the relationship between the Myers Briggs type indicator (MBTI) and NEO-PI five factor model of personality. *Personality and Individual Differences* 21: 303–7.

Glicksohn, J. & Rechtman, S. (2011) Profiling the profilers: who is watching our backs? *Personality and Individual Differences* 50: 755–8.

Gottman, J. M. (1994) *What Predicts Divorce? The Relationship between Marital Processes and Marital Outcomes*. Hilldale, NJ: Lawrence Erlbaum.

Grande, L. & Bayne, R. (2006) Adult dyslexia – the challenge to counsellors. *Therapy Today* (April): 31–4.

Guy, J. D. (1987) *The Personal Life of the Psychotherapist*. New York: Wiley.

Hartzler, G. & Hartzler, M. (2005) *Functions of Type. Activities to Develop the Eight Jungian Functions*. Huntingdon Beach, CA: Telos Publications.

Haslam, C., Jetten, J., Pugliese, C., Haslam, S. A. & Tonks, J. (2011) I remember therefore I am, and I am therefore I remember: analysis of the contributions of episodic and semantic self-knowledge to identity. *British Journal of Psychology* 10: 184–203.

Haslam, N. (2007) *Introduction to Personality and Intelligence*. London: Sage.

Hawkins, P. & Shohet, R. (2006) *Supervision in the Helping Professions*, 3rd edn. Oxford: Oxford University Press.

Hendrick, H. & Hendrick, S. S. (2006) Styles of romantic love. In R. J. Sternberg & K. Weis (eds), *The New Psychology of Love*. London: Yale University Press.

Hill, C. E. (2009) *Helping Skills. Facilitating Exploration, Insight, and Action*, 3rd edn. Washington, DC: American Psychological Association.

Hirsh, S. K. & Kummerow, J. M. (2000) *Introduction to Type in Organizations*, 3rd edn. Palo Alto, CA: CPP.

Jennings, L. & Skovholt, T. M. (1999) The cognitive, emotional and relational characteristics of master therapists. *Journal of Counseling Psychology* 46: 311.

Jetten, C., Haslam, C., Tonks, J. & Haslam, S. A. (2010) Declining autobiographical memory and the loss of identity: effects on wellbeing. *Journal of Clinical and Experimental Neuropsychology* 32: 408–16.

John, O. P. & Robins, R. W. (1994) Traits and types, dynamics and development: no doors should be closed in the study of personality. *Psychological Inquiry* 5: 137–42.

Jones, J. K. & Sherman, R. G. (2011) *Intimacy and Type. Building Enduring Relationships by Embracing Personality Differences*, 2nd edn. Gainesville, FL: CAPT.

Joseph, S. & Linley, A. P. (2006) *Positive Therapy. A Metatheory for Positive Psychological Practice*. London: Routledge.

Jourard, S. (1971) *The Transparent Self*, rev. edn. London: Van Nostrand Reinhold.

Judge, T. A., Livingston, B. A. & Hurst, C. (2012) Do nice guys – and gals – really finish last? The joint effects of sex and agreeableness on income. *Journal of Personality and Social Psychology* 102(2): 390–407.

Jung, C. G. (1923) *Psychological Types*. Princeton, NJ: Princeton University Press.

Jung, C. G. (1969) *Psychology and Religion: West and East*, 2nd edn. Princeton, NJ: Princeton University Press.

Keirsey, D. (1998) *Please Understand Me II*. Del Mar, CA: Prometheus Nemesis.

Kendall, E. (1998) *Myers Briggs Type Indicator: European English Edition Manual Supplement*. Oxford: OPP.

Kennedy-Moore, E. & Watson, J. C. (1999) *Expressing Emotion: Myths, Realities and Therapeutic Strategies*. London: Guilford Press.

Kern, M. L. & Friedman, H. S. (2008) Do conscientious individuals live longer? A quantitative review. *Health Psychology* 27(5): 505–12.

Kroeger, O. (1985) Fat is a typological issue. *The Type Reporter* 1: 16–17.

Kroeger, O. & Thuesen, J. M. (1988) *TypeTalk*. New York: Delacorte Press.

Kroeger, O. with Thuesen, J. M. & Rutledge, H. (2002) *Type Talk at Work*. New York: Dell Publishing.

Kummerow, J. M. (1998) Uses of type in careers counselling. In I. B. Myers, M. H. McCaulley, N. L. Quenk & A. L. Hammer (eds), *Manual: A Guide to the Development and Use of the Myers-Briggs Type Indicator*. Palo Alto, CA: CPP.

Kuncel, N. R., Ones, D. S. & Sackett, P. R. (2010) Individual differences as predictors of work, educational and broad life outcomes. *Personality and Individual Differences* 49: 331–6.

Lahey, B. B. (2009) Public health significance of neuroticism. *American Psychologist* 64: 241–56.

Lambert, M. J. & Shimokawa, K. (2011) Collecting client feedback. *Psychotherapy* 46: 729.

Lawrence, G. (1997) *Looking at Type and Learning Styles* Gainesville, FL: Center for Applications of Psychological Type.

Lawrence, G. (2009) *People Types and Tiger Stripes*, 4th edn. Gainesville, FL: Center for Applications of Psychological Type.

Lawrence, G. (2010) Refining the language of type descriptions. *Journal of Psychological Type* 12: 135–40.

Lawrence, G. & Martin, C. (2001) *Building People, Building Programs*. Gainesville, FL: Center for Applications of Psychological Type.

Lazarus, A. A. (1993) Tailoring the therapeutic relationship, or being an authentic chameleon. *Psychotherapy* 30: 404–7.

Lee, H. & Adams, T. (eds) (2011) *Creative Approaches in Dementia Care*. Basingstoke: Palgrave Macmillan.

Lee, J. A. (1988) Love-styles. In R. J. Sternberg & M. L. Barnes (eds), *The Psychology of Love*. London: Yale University Press.

Letzring, T. D. & Noftle, E. E. (2010) Predicting relationship quality from self-verification of broad personality traits among romantic couples. *Journal of Research in Personality* 44: 353–62.

Lilgendahl, J. P. & McAdams, D. P. (2011) Constructing stories of self-growth: how individual differences in patterns of autobiographical reasoning relate to well-being in midlife. *Journal of Personality* 79: 391–428.

Linley, A. (2008) *Average to A+. Realising Strengths in Yourself and Others*. Coventry: CAPP Press.

Lively, P. (1998) *Spiderweb*. London: Penguin.

Lloyd, J. B. (2008) Myers-Briggs theory: how true? how necessary? *Journal of Psychological Type* 68: 43–50.

Lloyd, J. B. (2012) The Myers-Briggs Type Indicator and mainstream psychology: analysis and evaluation of an unresolved hostility. *Journal of Beliefs and Values* 33: 23–34.

Lyubomirsky, S., Sousa, L. & Dickerhoof, R. (2006) The costs and benefits of writing, talking and thinking about life's triumphs and defeats. *Journal of Personality and Social Psychology* 90: 692–708.

McAdams, D. P. (1995) What do we know when we know a person? *Journal of Personality* 63(3): 365–96.

McAdams, D. P. (2006) *The Person. An Introduction to the Science of Personality Psychology*, 4th edn. Chichester: Wiley.

McAdams, D. P. (2009) *The Person: An Introduction to the Science of Personality*, 5th edn. Chichester: Wiley.

McAdams, D. P. & Pals, J. L. (2006) A new Big Five: fundamental principles for an integrative science of personality. *American Psychologist* 61: 204–17.

McCaulley, M. (1996) Traversing the S N chasm. *Bulletin of Psychological Type* 19: 22–4.

McCrae, R. R. & Costa, P. T. (1989) Re-interpreting the Myers Briggs type indicator from the perspective of the five factor model of personality. *Journal of Personality* 57: 17–37.

McLeod, J. (2009) *An Introduction to Counselling*, 4th edn. Milton Keynes: Open University Press.

Magee, C. A & Heaven, P. C. L. (2011) Big-Five personality factors, obesity and 2 year weight gain in Australian adults. *Journal of Research in Personality* 45: 332–5.

Malouff, G. M., Thorsteinsson, E. B., Schutte, N. S., Bhullar, N. & Rooke, S. E. (2010) The Five-Factor Model of personality and relationship satisfaction of intimate partners: a meta-analysis. *Journal of Research in Personality* 44: 124–7.

Maslow, A. H. (1968) *Toward a Psychology of Being*, 2nd edn. New York: Van Nostrand Reinhold.

Matthews, G., Deary, I. J. & Whiteman, M. C. (2009) *Personality Traits*, 3rd edn. Cambridge: Cambridge University Press.

Mearns, D. & Thorne, B. (2007) *Person-Centred Counselling in Action*, 3rd edn. London: Sage.

Mehl, M. R., Gosling, S. D. & Pennebaker, J. W. (2006) Personality in its natural habitat: manifestations and implicit folk theories of personality in daily life. *Journal of Personality and Social Psychology* 90: 862–77.

Miller, T. (1991) The psychotherapeutic utility of the five-factor model of personality: a clinician's experience. *Journal of Personality Assessment* 57: 415–33.

Mount, M. K. & Barrick, M. R. (1998) Five reasons why the Big Five article has been frequently cited. *Personnel Psychology* 51: 849–57.

Murphy, E. (1992) *The Developing Child: Using Jungian Type to Understand Children*. Palo Alto, CA: CPP.

Murray, W. D. G. (1995) *Give Yourself the Unfair Advantage*. Gladwyne, PA: Type and Temperament.

Myers, I. B. (with Myers, P. B.) (1980) *Gifts Differing*. Palo Alto, CA: CPP.

Myers, I. B. (with Myers, K. & Kirby, L.) (1998) *Introduction to Type*, 5th edn. Oxford: OPP.

Myers, I. B. & McCaulley, M. H. (1985) *Manual: A Guide to the Development and Use of the Myers-Briggs Type Indicator*, 2nd edn. Palo Alto, CA: CPP.

Myers, I. B., McCaulley, M. H., Quenk, N. L. & Hammer, A. L. (1998) *Manual: A Guide to the Development and Use of the Myers-Briggs Type Indicator*, 3rd edn. Palo Alto, CA: CPP.

Myers, K. D. & Kirby, L. K. (1994) *Introduction to Type Dynamics and Type Development*. Palo Alto, CA: CPP.

Myerson, J. (1994) *Sleepwalking*. London: Picador.

Nardi, D. (1999) *Character and Personality Type: Discovering your Uniqueness for Career and Relationship Success*. Huntingdon Beach, CA: Telos Publications.

Nehrer, A. (1996) Jung's theory of archetypes: a critique. *Journal of Humanistic Psychology* 36: 61–91.

Nettle, D. (2007) *Personality*. Oxford: Oxford University Press.

Nicolson, P. & Bayne, R. (in press) *Psychology for Social Work Theory and Practice*. Basingstoke: Palgrave Macmillan.

Nocita, A. & Stiles, W. B. (1986) Client introversion and counseling session impact. *Journal of Counseling Psychology* 33: 270–3.

Norcross, J. C., Krebs, P. M. & Prochaska, J. D. (2011) Stages of change. *Journal of Clinical Psychology: In Session* 67: 143–54.

Norcross, J. C. & Wampold, B. E. (2011a) Evidence-based therapy relationships: research conclusions and clinical practices. *Psychotherapy* 46: 98–102.

Norcross, J. C. & Wampold, B. E. (2011b) What works for whom: tailoring psychotherapy to the person. *Journal of Clinical Psychology: In Session* 67(2): 127–32.

Ogles, B. M., Lambert, M. J. & Ogles, B. M. (2004) The efficacy and effectiveness of psychotherapy. In M. J. Lambert (ed.), *Bergin and Garfield's Handbook of Psychotherapy and Behaviour Change*, 5th edn. Chichester: Wiley.

Okiishi, J., Lambert, M. J., Nielsen, S. I. & Ogles, B. M. (2003) Waiting for supershrink: an empirical analysis of therapists effects. *Clinical Psychology and Psychotherapy* 10: 361–73.

Ozer, D. J. & BenetMartinez, V. (2006) Personality and the prediction of consequential outcomes. *Annual Review of Psychology* 57: 401–21.

Patrick, E. (2003) Values? Now where did I put them? *Counselling and Psychotherapy Journal* (August): 30–1.

Pearson, C. S. & Marr, H. K. (2007) *What Story Are You Living?* Gainesville, FL: Center for Applications for Psychological Type.

Penley, J. P. with Eble, D. (2006) *MotherStyles. Using Personality Type to Discover Your Parenting Strengths*. Cambridge, MA: Da Capo Press.

Pennebaker, J. W. (2012) *The Secret Life of Pronouns*. London: Bloomsbury Press.

Pennebaker, J. W., Colder, M. & Sharp, L. K. (1990) Accelerating the coping process. *Journal of Personality and Social Psychology* 58: 528–37.

Penner, R. (1992) Applying type in adapting to chronic illness. *Bulletin of Psychological Type* 15: 15–16.

Pinker, S. (2002) *The Blank Slate*. London: Allen Lane.

Pratt, C. D. & Gray, P. (1999) Bridging the SN chasm. *APT XIII Conference Proceedings*, 957. Minneapolis, MN: Association for Psychological Type.

Prinzi, P., Stams, G. J. J. M., Dekovic, M., Reijntjes, A. H. A. & Belsky, J. (2009) The relations between parents' Big Five personality factors and parenting: a meta-analytic review. *Journal of Personality and Social Psychology* 97: 351–62.

Provost, J. A. (1993) *Applications of the Myers-Briggs Type Indicator in Counseling: A Casebook*, 2nd edn. Gainesville, FL: CAPT.

Quenk, N. L. (1996) *In the Grip: Our Hidden Personality*. Palo Alto, CA: Consulting Psychologists Press.

Quenk, N. L. (2002) *Was That Really Me?* Palo Alto, CA: Davies-Black.

Quenk, N. L. & Kummerow, J. M. (2011) *MBTI Step II User's Guide*. Palo Alto, CA: CPP.

Raggatt, P. (2006) Putting the five-factor model into context: evidence linking Big Five traits to narrative identity. *Journal of Personality* 74: 1321–47.

Rammstedt, B. & Schupp, J (2008) Only the congruent survive – personality similarities in couples. *Personality and Individual Differences* 45: 533–6.

Rauch, J. (2003) Caring for your introvert. *The Atlantic Monthly* 291: 133–4.

Reynierse, J. H. (2009) The case against type dynamics. *Journal of Psychological Type* 69: 129.

Reynierse, J. H. (2012) Toward an empirically sound and radically revised type theory. *Journal of Psychological Type* 72: 125.

Roberts, B. W., Kuncel, N. R., Shiner, R., Caspi, A. & Goldberg, L. R. (2007) The power of personality. The comparative validity of personality traits, socioeconomic status, and cognitive ability for predicting important life outcomes. *Perspectives on Psychological Science* 2(4): 313–45.

Rogers, C. R. (1961) *On Becoming a Person: A Therapist's View of Psychotherapy*. London: Constable.

Romero, E., Villar, P., Luengo, M. A. & Gomez-Fraguela, J. A. (2009) Traits, personal strivings and well-being. *Journal of Research in Personality* 43: 535–46.

Rutter, M. (2006) *Genes and Behavior. Nature–Nurture Interplay Explained*. Oxford: Blackwell.

Scanlon, S. (1986) A matter of taste ... and type. *The Type Reporter* 2: 210.

Shields, C. (1976) *Small Ceremonies*. London: Fourth Estate.

Shields, C. (1977) *The Box Garden*. London: Fourth Estate.

Singer, J. A. (2005) *Personality and Psychotherapy. Treating the Whole Person*. London: The Guilford Press.

Smith, V., Collard, P., Nicolson, P. & Bayne, R. (2012) *Key Concepts in Counselling and Psychotherapy. A Critical A–Z Guide to Theory*. Buckingham: Open University Press, McGraw Hill Education.

Steiner, C. (1974) *Scripts People Live*. New York: Bantam Books.

Sternberg, R. J. & Weis, K. (2006) *The New Psychology of Love*. London: Yale University Press.

Stokes, J. (1987a) Exploring the relationship of type and gender. Part 1: Anecdotal experiences of MBTI users. *Journal of Psychological Type* 13: 34–43.

Stokes, J. (1987b) Exploring the relationship of type and gender. Part 2: A review and critique of empirical research and other data. *Journal of Psychological Type* 13: 44–51.

Sutin, A. R., Ferrucci, L., Zonderman, A. B. & Terracciano, A. (2011) Personality and obesity across the adult lifespan. *Journal of Personality and Social Psychology* 101: 579–92.

Swift, J. K., Callahan, J. L. & Vollmer, B. M. (2011) Preferences. *Journal of Clinical Psychology: In Session* 67: 155–65.

Thompson, H. L. (1996) *Jung's Function – Attitudes Explained*. Watkinsville, GA: Wormhole Publications.

Tieger, P. D. & Barron-Tieger, B. (2000) *Just Your Type: The Relationship You've Always Wanted Using the Secrets of Personality Type*. London: Little, Brown.

Tieger, P. D. & Barron-Tieger, B. (2007) *Do What You Are*, 4th edn. London: Little, Brown.

Topolinski, S. & Hertel, G. (2007) The role of personality in psychotherapists' careers: relationships between personality traits, therapeutic schools, and job satisfaction. *Psychotherapy Research* 17: 378–90.

Tryon, G. S. & Winograd, G. (2011) Goal consensus and collaboration. *Psychotherapy* 48(1): 50–7.

VanSant, S. (2003) *Wired for Conflict: The Role of Personality in Resolving Differences*. Gainesville, FL: CAPT.

Vazire, S. (2010) Who knows what about a person? The self–other knowledge asymmetry (SOKA) model. *Journal of Personality and Social Psychology* 98: 281–300.

Vollrath, M. & Torgersen, S (2000) Personality types and coping. *Personality and Individual Differences* 29: 367–78.

Vollrath, M. & Torgersen, S. (2002) Who takes health risks? A probe into eight personality types. *Personality and Individual Differences* 32: 1185–97.

Walsh, P. (2008) *Does This Clutter Make My Butt Look Fat? The Easy Weight-Loss Plan*. New York: Simon and Schuster.

Wampold, B. E. (2007) Psychotherapy: the humanistic (and effective) treatment. *American Psychologist* (November): 857–73.

Weakes, W., McLeod, J. & Wilkinson, H. (2006) Dementia. *Therapy Today* (April): 12–15.

Wennik, R. S. (1999) *Your Personality Prescription*. New York: Kensington Books.

White, H. A. & Shah, P. (2011) Creative style and achievement in adults with attention-deficit/hyperactivity disorder. *Personality and Individual Differences* 50: 673–7.

Whitemore, R. & Dixon, J. (2008) Chronic illness: the process of integration. *Journal of Nursing and Healthcare of Chronic Illness* in association with *Journal of Clinical Nursing* 17: 177–87.

Widiger, T. A. & Costa, P. T. (in press) Integrating normal and abnormal personality structure: The five factor model. *Journal of Personality*.

Wiebe, D. J., Drew, L. M & Croom, A. (2010) Personality, health and illness. In D. French, K. Vedhara, A. A., Kaptein & J. Weinman (eds), *Health Psychology*, 2nd edn. Oxford: BPS Blackwell.

Williams, S. L. & French, D. P. (2011) What are the most effective intervention techniques for changing physical activity self-efficacy and physical activity behaviour – and are they the same? *Health Education Research* 26: 308–22.

Willingham, D. T. (2007) *Cognition. The Thinking Animal*, 3rd edn. Upper Saddle River, NJ: Pearson Education.

Winter, D. J., John, O. P., Stuart, A. J., Klohnen, E. C. & Duncan, L. E. (1998) Traits and motives: toward and integration of two traditions in personality research. *Psychological Review* 105: 230–50.

Worden, J. W. (2008) *Grief Counselling and Grief Therapy: A Handbook for the Mental Health Practitioner*. New York: Springer.

Wortman, C. B. & Silver, R. C. (1989) The myths of coping with loss. *Journal of Clinical and Counselling Psychology* 57: 349–57.

Yalom, I. D. (2001) *The Gift of Therapy. Reflections on Being a Therapist*. London: Piatkus.

Zeisset, C. (2006) *The Art of Dialogue. Exploring Personality Differences for More Effective Communication*. Gainesville, FL: Center For Applications of Psychological Type.

Index

Page numbers in *italics* denote a table/diagram

acceptance   80–2
agreeableness   *14*
Allen, Judy   71, 112
anxiety   43
  and Big Five theory   *14*
  reframing of as two preferences   14–15, 25
  strengths of   14–15
archetypes   135–7, *137*
Aron, Elaine   38, 79, 96
Asperger's syndrome   116
assertiveness skills   88
astrology   47–8
Attention Deficit Disorder (ADD)   115–16
Attention Deficit Hyperactivity Disorder (ADHD)   115–16
authentic chameleon issue   70, 73–4
auxiliary function   119

bad news
  receiving and adapting to   112–13
Barger, N.   77
Barnes, Simon   80–1
Barrick, M. R.   99
Barron-Tieger, Barbara   100
Bayne, Rowan   39, 64, 118, 119
Berens, Linda   43, 50–1, 65
Berne, E.   134
Big Five (five factor theory)   13–20, *14*, 38, 76, 77, 111
  and anxiety   14–15

comparison with preference theory   15–20
factors and meanings   *14*
questionnaires for measuring   42
and tone   16–17, *17*
validity   15–16
Bonanno, G. A.   113–14
boundaries, maintaining   8
box, being put in a   46–7
Boyd, William
  Any Human Heart   133
brainstorming   102
Briggs, Katherine   52
Brock, Susan   34, 71, 85, 112
Brue, Suzanne   111
Buss, A. H.   76

Calm (C) preference   14–15, 96
  associated strengths and weaknesses of counsellors   62
  characteristics associated with   36–8, *37*
  communicating with clients who prefer   78–9
  communication problems with Worrying preference and strategies for managing   *90*, *91*
  negative perceptions of   *81*
  strategies for developing   24
  stress and coping strategies   *107*, *108*
  and work   99
  writing strategies for   86
Carr, Sally   27, 29–30

151

case studies   29–30, 118–30
CBT (cognitive behavioural therapy)   76, 138
   preferences of experienced counsellors in   64, 65
ceiling effects   22
Centre for Applied Positive Psychology   69
Cheek, J. M.   76
child rearing   97
childhood   39, 133–4
Chronic Fatigue Syndrome (ME)   113
Churchill, Susy   83, 105
client–counsellor relationship *see* counsellor–client relationship
cognitive behavioural therapy *see* CBT
collaboration   5, 8
collective unconscious   136
communication
   with clients of each preference   75–9
   and four temperaments   92
   and prediction of divorce   96
   problems with opposed preferences   89–90, *90*
   strategies for managing problems between opposed preferences   *91*
conscientiousness   99
   and Big Five theory   *14*
   and job selection   99
   and longevity   15–16
constructivism   48, 132, 137–8
contemplation   72
Corey, Gerald   60
Costa, P. T.   15, 16
counselling
   research on effectiveness of   4–5
counselling model
   motives and your choice of   61, 63–4, *64*
   three-stage model   61, 63, 72, 73
counselling qualities   80–5
   acceptance   80–2
   empathy   82–3
   genuineness   84–5
counselling room   86–7

counsellor–client relationship   70–87
   and authentic chameleon issue   73–4
   and collaboration   5, 8
   collecting feedback and the skill of immediacy   74–5
   communicating with clients of each preference   75–9
   core counselling qualities   80–5
   and counselling room   86–7
   improving   8–9
   ISFJ case study   79
   and marketing yourself as a counsellor   85–6
   matching counsellors and clients   5, 8, 71–5
   matching languages   71–2
   and stages of change model   72–3
counsellors
   idea of 'good'   61
   marketing yourself   85–6
   motives for becoming   60–1
cultures, preference theory and different   47
CVs   100

Daily Diary Completions   32
Darker, C. D.   105
dementia   116–17
depression
   'bright side' of   37
   treatment of   37
detective work   27, 29
distress, during and after counselling   75–6
divorce, communication predicting   96
Dixon, J.   114
Dodd, Nick   64
dominant function   118
Dosani, Sabina   116
Dryden, Windy   63–4, 73, 75
Duncan, B. L.   74
Dunn, Sophia   114–15
dyslexia   116

effective practice, characteristics of 23
EFJ type 59
EFSP type
  characteristics 56–7
  motives and values 57
Electronically Activated Recorders
  (EAR) 32
Emmons, R. A. 65
empathy 5, 8, 82–3
ENFJ type
  brief description 45
  characteristics 55
  motives and values 55–6
ENFP type
  brief description 45
  characteristics 58
  and counsellor–client
    relationship 78, 79–80
  motives and values 58–9
  strengths and weaknesses 18–19
ENP type 59
  and ADHD/ADD 116
ENTJ type
  brief description 45
  characteristics 53
  motives and values 52
ENTP type 29–30
  brief description 45
  characteristics 57
  motives and values 57–8
EP type
  and love styles 93
Ericsson, K. A. 22
ESFJ type 48
  brief description 45
  characteristics 54
  motives and values 54–5
ESFP type
  brief description 45
  characteristics 56–7
  motives and values 57
ESP type 59
ESTJ type 48
  brief description 45
  characteristics 54

  motives and values 54
ESTJ type case study 118, 119–28
  extraverted Thinking (dominant
    function) 120–1
  introverted Feeling (inferior
    function) 124–7
  introverted Sensing (auxiliary
    function) 121–3
  Intuition (tertiary function) 123–4
ESTP type
  brief description 45
  characteristics 56
  motives and values 56
  and work 99
ETJ type 59
exercise 105, 106, 111–12, *112*
exercises, brief 39
Extraversion (E) preference 9–10, 26,
    29, 73, 95
  associated strengths and weaknesses of
    counsellors 62
  association with obesity and weight
    gain 106
  and Big Five theory 14
  brief description 11
  characteristics associated with 33–4, *33*
  communicating with clients
    with 75–6
  communication problems with
    Introverts and strategies for
    managing 89–90, *90*, *91*
  and exercise 111
  learning styles associated with *102*
  negative perceptions of 81
  and shyness 76
  strategies for developing 24
  stress and coping strategies *107*, *108*
  writing strategies for 86
extrinsic motivation 50

Faber, M. A. 136, 137
falsification of type 21, 70
feedback 5
  collecting of and skill of
    immediacy 74–5

Feeling (F) preference 10, 66, 95
  associated strengths and weaknesses of counsellors 62
  brief description 11
  characteristics associated with 35, *35*
  communicating with clients with 77
  communication problems with Thinking preference and strategies for managing 90, *91*
  learning styles associated with *102*
  men with 77
  negative perceptions of *81*
  strategies for developing 24
  stress and coping strategies 107, *108*
  writing strategies for 86
five factor theory *see* Big Five
Fleeson, W. 32–3
flooding 139
force-field analysis 105
four 'languages' 71–2
Freud, Sigmund 5
Friedman, H. S. 15
function-attitudes 23, 118–19
Furnham, A. 15

Gallagher, P. 32–3
genetic influences and personality 39, 48
genuineness 84–5
Gladwell, Malcolm 22
'good counsellor' 61, *62–3*
Gottman, J. M. 96
grief 113–14
Guy, J. D. 60

Haslam, Cathy 117
Hawkins, P. 60
health 104–17
  and exercise 105, 106, 111–12, *112*
  and losing weight 109–11, *110*
  and loss 113–14
  receiving and adapting to 'bad news' 112–13
  stress *see* stress
  tiredness 106–7
  see also mental health

health promotion campaigns 106
Heaven, P. C. I. 106
Hertel, G. 63
high neuroticism 79, 96
Highly Sensitive Person (HSP) 38–9, 108
Hirsh, S. K. 43
humanistic 138

identical twins 48
IFP type *59*
immediacy, use of skill of 74–5
implicit observation 30–1
inactivity 105–6
INFJ type 48
  brief description 44
  and CBT counsellors 64
  characteristics 56
  motives and values 56
INFP type 67
  brief description 44
  and CBT counsellors 64
  characteristics 52, *54*
  motives and values *54*
  and work 99–100
INFPC type case study 118, 128–30
  appealing and repelling activities 129
  love of sport 129
  love of words 128–9
  other preferences and non-preferences 130
  time alone 130
INJ type *59*
inferior/fourth function 119
International Association for Psychological Type Conference (1985) 119
interview
  job 100
  life story 134–5
INTJ type 30, 48
  brief description 44
  and CBT counsellors 64
  characteristics 56–7
  motives and values 57
  and work 99

INTP type
  brief description 44
  characteristics 54
  motives and values 54–5
  and personality disorder 115
  and women 77
intrinsic motivation 50
Introduction to Type 43
Introversion (I) preference 7, 9–10, 17, 26, 29, 95
  associated strengths and weaknesses of counsellors 62
  brief description 11
  characteristics associated with 33–4, *33*
  communicating with clients with 75–6
  communication problems with Extraverts and strategies for managing 89–90, *90*, *91*
  and exercise 111
  learning styles associated with 102
  negative perceptions of 81
  and parenting 97
  strategies for developing 24
  stress and coping strategies *107*, *108*
  writing strategies for 86
Intuition (N) preference 10, 11, 73, 95
  associated strengths and weaknesses of counsellors 62
  brief description 11
  characteristics associated with 34–5, *34*
  communicating with clients with 76
  and exercise 111
  learning styles associated with 102–3, *102*
  negative perceptions of 81
  picture exercise 39
  strategies for developing 24
  stress and coping strategies *107*, *108*
  writing strategies for 86
ISFJ type 48
  brief description 44
  characteristics 57
  counsellor–client relationship case study 79
  motives and values 57–8

ISFP type
  brief description 44
  characteristics 53
  motives and values 53
  and work 100
ISJ type 59
ISTJ type 48, 67
  brief description 44
  characteristics 58
  motives and values 58–9
ISTP type
  brief description 44
  characteristics 55
  motives and values 55–6
ITP type 59

Jennings, L. 61
Jones, J. K. 95
Jourard, Sidney 6
Judging (J) preference 10, 15–16, 80, 96
  associated strengths and weaknesses of counsellors 62
  brief description 11
  characteristics associated with 35–6, *36*
  communicating with clients with 78
  communication problems with Perceiving preference and strategies for managing 90, *90*, *91*
  and exercise 111
  learning styles associated with 102
  and making lists 32
  and ME 113
  negative perceptions of 81
  strategies for developing 24
  stress and coping strategies *107*, *108*
  and time management 101
  writing strategies for 86
Jung, Carl 23, 28, 53, 135–6

Keirsey, D. 39–42, 43, 93
Keirsey Temperament Sorter II 42
Kendall, E. 48
Kennedy-Moore, E. 139
Ker, M. L. 15
Kirby, Linda 22, 59, 77

kissing   94–5
Kroeger, Otto   43, 51–2, 77, 95, 107
Kummerow, Jean   43, 98, 99, 118–28

laddering   68
Lambert, M. J.   74
languages, matching   71–2
Lawrence, Gordon   39, 43, 52–3, *53–9*
Lazarus, Arnold   73
learning styles   102–3, *102*
Lee, John   92–3, 94
life stories   3–4, *4*, 18, 116, 131–9
   analysing and reconstructing   137–9
   and archetypes   135–7, *137*
   how and when to suggest exploring   132–3
   interview   134–5
   and mental and physical health   132
   methods for exploring   133–7
   and scripts   133–4
   and self-defining memories   134
Lift   69
Linley, Alex   10, 68, 69
Lively, Penelope
   Spiderweb   90
Lloyd, John   17
longevity
   and conscientiousness   15–16
loss   113–14
love   92–7
   communicating that predicts divorce   96
   kissing   94
   lasting relationships   96–7
   Lee's styles of   92–5, *93*
   marriage and similarity in personality   97
   potential problems between people with the same preferences   95–6
   recovering   95
   and sex   94–5
   Sternberg's model of   93

McAdams, Dan   5, 18, 132, 134
   integrative model of personality   1–4, 131

'What do we know when we know a person?'   1
McCaulley, Mary   103
McCrae, R. R.   15, 16
McLeod, John   138
Magee, C. A.   106
maintenance   72
marketing, of yourself as counsellor   85–6
Marr, H. K.   137
marriage
   and similarity of personality   97
Martin, C.   39
Maslow, Abraham   6, 84
'master therapists'   61
Matthews, G.   34
Mayer, J. D.   136, 137
MBTI (Myers-Briggs Type Indicator)   12, 13, 23, 25, 29, 42, 47, 114, 115, 118
ME (Chronic Fatigue Syndrome)   113
Mearns, Dave   28, 84
Mehl, M. R.   34
memories, self-defining   135
mental health   105, 114–17
   Attention Deficit Hyperactivity Disorder and Attention Deficit Disorder   115–16
   dementia   116–17
   and having a good life story   132
   personality disorders   114–15
Miller, Jonathan   90
Miller, Timothy   76, 77, 78, 79, 108, 109–10
Mothers of Many Styles (M.O.M.S.)   97
motivation
   intrinsic versus extrinsic   50
motives   3, 4, *4*, 18, 49–69
   for becoming a counsellor   60–1
   definition   49–50
   and discovering personal strivings   65–7
   methods for discovering   67–8
   and preferences   52–60, *53–9*
   and temperament theory   50–2, *51*
   and traits   49

and your choice of counselling
    model   61, 63–4, *64*
Mount, M. K.   99
mourning   114
Murphy, Elizabeth   97
Murray, W. D. G.   32
Myers, Isabel   21, 23, 43, 52, 84
Myers, Katherine   22, 59
Myers, P. B.   21
Myers-Briggs Type Indicator *see* MBTI

Nardi, D.   43, 51
National Institute for Health and
    Clinical Excellence (NICE)   116
negative emotions   37
Nehrer, A.   136
Nettle, Daniel   14–15, 34, 37, 42
NF language   71
NF temperament   39, 52, 71
    and communication   92
    core motives in   *51*
    and losing weight   *110*, 111
    love styles   93
    and ME   113
    and occupations   98–9
    reaction to stress   *107*
    stick figures   *41*
NJ preference
    and time management   *102*
Nocita, A.   75–6
non-preferences   19, 20, 21, 22
non-verbal communication   71
Norcross, J. C.   5, 73, 74, 133
'not knowing' stance   138
NP preference
    and time management   *102*
NT language   71
NT temperament   39, 52, 93
    and communication   92
    core motives in   *51*
    and losing weight   *110*, 111
    and ME   113
    and occupations   98
    reaction to stress   *107*
    stick figure   *41*

obesity   105, 106
observation, implicit   30–1
O'Hagan, Sean   36
openness   *14*
optimism   37–8

parenting   97
Patrick, Eleanor   68
Pearson, C. S.   137
Pearson–Marr Archetype Indicator   137
Penley, Janet   97
Pennebaker, James   132, 139
Penner, Ron   113
Perceiving (P) preference   10, 15, *17*,
    73, 80, 96
    associated strengths and weaknesses of
        counsellors   62
    association with obesity and weight
        gain   106
    bias against and negative perceptions
        of   80, *81*
    brief description   *11*
    characteristics associated with   35–6,
        36
    communicating with clients with   78
    communication problems with
        Judgement preference and strategies
        for managing   90, *90*, *91*
    and exercise   111
    learning styles associated with   *102*
    and losing weight   109–10, 111
    and making lists   32
    and ME   113
    strategies for developing   24
    stress and coping strategies   *107*, *108*
    and time management   101
    and work   99
    writing strategies for   86
personal strivings   65–7
personality change   20–2
personality clashes   88
personality development   18–20
personality disorders   114–15
Pinker, Steven
    The Blank Slate   48

positive psychology 14
Pratt, Chuck 102–3
precontemplation 72
preference envy 82
preference theory/preferences 2–3, 4, *4*, 7, 8, 9–13, 20
  and brief exercises 39
  case studies 29–30
  and choice of orientation 61, 63–4, *64*, *65*
  clarifying of each 31–9
  communication and problems with opposed 89–91, *90*, *91*
  comparison with Big Five theory 15–18
  concept of 'preference' 9–11
  concept of 'psychological type' 11–13
  definition 9
  and different cultures 47
  discovering the 27–48
  emphasis on strengths 10, 17
  environmental factors impeding 19
  experiment with behaving as if you have each preference 46
  and health 104–17
  and idea of 'good counsellor' 61, *62*–3
  and improving the counselling–client relationship 70–87
  and learning styles 102–3, *102*
  and love 93–7
  and motives 52–60, *53*–9
  numbers of people with specific types 48
  overview of counsellors' use of 24–5
  and parenting 97
  and personality change 20–1
  and personality development 18–19
  positivity of 16, 17
  principles for discovering 28–9
  principles and strategies for developing 22–4, *24*
  and questionnaires 42
  questions about and replies 46–8
  single-letter abbreviations summary 26

  stability of 18
  strategies in a counselling session 30–48
  and tone 16–17, *17*
  types and descriptions 10, *11*, 42–3, 44–5
  validity 15–16
  and versatility 17–18
  and work 98–103
preparation 72
profiles 12–13
Provost, Judy 72, 76, 78, 79–80
psychodynamic 138
psychological death 50–1, 65
psychological type 9, 11–13 *see also* preference theory/preferences
public speaking 103

Quenk, Naomi 23
questionnaires
  measures of personality 42
  and strengths 69, 100
  see also MBTI

Rauch, Jonathan 89
real self 6, 7, 48, 84, 134
realist view 132
REBT (rational emotive behaviour therapy) 63, 77
redundancy 103
referral 75
Reynierse, Jim 12–13
Richards, Keith 36
Rogers, Carl 6, 73, 84

Scanlon, Susan 110
scripts 133–4
self-actualisation 84, 115
self-alienation 84
self-awareness 5–8, *6*, 84
self-defining memories 134
Sensing (S) preference 10, *17*, 39, 95
  associated strengths and weaknesses of counsellors 62
  brief description *11*

INDEX **159**

  characteristics associated with   34–5, *34*
  communicating with clients with   76
  communication problems with
    Intuition preference and strategies for managing   90, *91*
  and exercise   111
  learning styles associated with   102–3, *102*
  negative perceptions of   *81*
  and parenting   97
  picture exercise   39
  strategies for developing   24
  stress and coping strategies   *107, 108*
  writing strategies for   86
sex   94–5
SF language   71
shadow side   23
Sherman, R. G.   95
Shields, Carol
  The Box Garden   19–20
  Small Ceremonies   19, 20
Shimokawa, K.   74
Shohet, R.   60
shy Extraverts   76
Silver, R. C.   113
Singer, J. A.   65, 66, 138
SJ temperament   39, 52, 64, 82, 85
  and CBT counsellors   64
  and communication   92
  core motives in   *51*
  and losing weight   *110*, 111
  love styles   93
  and ME   113
  and occupations   98
  reaction to stress   *107*
  stick figure   *40*
  and time management   *102*
Skovholt, T. M.   61
smoke detectors   37
SP temperament   39, 52, 85
  and ADHD/ADD   116
  and communication   92
  core motives in   *51*
  and losing weight   *110*

  and ME   113
  and occupations   98
  reaction to stress   *107*
  stick figure   *40*
  and time management   *102*
'sparkling moments'   138
ST language   71
stages of change model   72–3, 105
Sternberg, Robert   93
Stiles, W. N.   75–6
strengths   10, 68–9
  emphasis on in preference theory   10, 17
  and questionnaire   69, 100
stress   105, 106–9, *107*
  coping with   108–9
  and eight personality types   107–8, *109*
  and preferences   *107*
  preferences and coping with   106–7, *108*
  temperament theory and reaction to   *107*
Strivings Assessment Questionnaire (SAQ)   50, 65–6
Sutin, A. R.   106, 111
Swift, J. K.   74

talent   22, 23
Taylor, Laurie   90
temperament theory   39–42, 61, 82, 83
  and ADHD/ADD   115–16
  and communication   92
  and losing weight   110, *110*
  and ME   113
  and motives   50–2, *51*
  and reaction to stress   *107*
  stick figures   40–1
  and work   98–9
'ten year rule'   22
tertiary function   119
therapist–patient relationship *see* counsellor–client relationship
Thinking (T) preference   10, *17*, 95
  associated strengths and weaknesses of counsellors   62

Thinking (T) preference – *continued*
  brief description 11
  characteristics associated with 35, *35*
  communicating with clients with 77
  communication problems with
    Feeling preference and strategies for
    managing 90, *91*
  learning styles associated with *102*
  negative perceptions of *81*
  strategies for developing 24
  stress and coping strategies *107, 108*
  and women 77
  writing strategies for *86*
Thorne, Brian 28, 84
three-stage model of counselling 61, 63, 72, 73
Thuesen, J. M. 43, 51–2, 77
tidiness/untidiness 80–1
Tieger, Paul 100
time management 100–2, *102*
tiredness 106–7
Topolinski, S. 63
Torgersen, S. 108
traits 2–3, 17, 32–3, 49 *see also* preference theory/preferences
traumatic stories 132–3, 139
Tryon, G. S. 5
type dynamics 12, 23, 53, 59, 118
type falsification 21, 70
types 11–13
  defence of term 11–12
  descriptions 42–3, *44–5*
  most/least frequent figures *48*
  Reynierse's meaning of 12–13

values 68, *69*
VanSant, S. 71, 91
versatility 73–4
Vollrath, M. 108

walking 105
Walsh, P.
  Does This Clutter Make My Butt Look Fat? 80

Wampold, Bruce 5, 8, 74, 133
Watson, J. C. 139
weight, losing 109–11, *110*
Wennik, R. S. 32
Whitemore, R. 114
Willingham, D. T. 22
Winograd, G. 5
Winter, D. J. 49
women
  and Thinking preference 77
Worden, J. W. 114
work 98–103
  and conscientiousness 99
  CV improvement 100
  interview technique 100
  learning styles 102–3
  and redundancy 103
  speaking in meetings 103
  and temperament theory 98–9
  and time management 100–1
Worrying (W) preference 14, 15, 22, 66, 96
  associated strengths and weaknesses of counsellors *62*
  characteristics associated with 36–9, *37*
  communicating with clients with 78–9
  communication problems with
    Calm preference and strategies for
    managing 90, *91*
  and Highly Sensitive Person (HSP) 38–9
  love styles *93*
  negative perceptions of *81*
  strategies for developing 24
  stress and coping strategies *107, 108*
  and work 99
  writing strategies for *86*
Wortman, C. B. 113
writing materials for clients *86*

Yalom, Irwin 139

Zeisset, C. 91